BUSINESS ISSUES, COMPETITION AND ENTREPRENEURSHIP

MANAGED 401(K) ACCOUNTS

ADVANTAGES, DISADVANTAGES, ISSUES

Business Issues, Competition and Entrepreneurship

Additional books in this series can be found on Nova's website under the Series tab.

Additional e-books in this series can be found on Nova's website under the e-book tab.

BUSINESS ISSUES, COMPETITION AND ENTREPRENEURSHIP

MANAGED 401(K) ACCOUNTS

ADVANTAGES, DISADVANTAGES, ISSUES

HAROLD PARKER
EDITOR

nova publishers
New York

For permission to use material from this book please contact us:
Telephone 631-231-7269; Fax 631-231-8175
Web Site: http://www.novapublishers.com

Additional color graphics may be available in the e-book version of this book.

Library of Congress Cataloging-in-Publication Data

ISBN: 978-1-63463-592-9

Published by Nova Science Publishers, Inc. † New York

CONTENTS

PREFACE

This book examines how providers structure managed accounts; their advantages and disadvantages for participants; and challenges sponsors face in selecting and overseeing providers.

Chapter 1 – 401(k) plan sponsors have increasingly offered participants managed accounts—*services* under which providers manage participants' 401(k) savings over time by making investment and portfolio decisions for them. These services differ from investment options offered within 401(k) plans. Because little is known about whether managed accounts are advantageous for participants and whether sponsors understand their own role and potential risks, GAO was asked to review these services.

GAO examined (1) how providers structure managed accounts, (2) their advantages and disadvantages for participants, and (3) challenges sponsors face in selecting and overseeing providers. In conducting this work, GAO reviewed relevant federal laws and regulations and surveyed plan sponsors. GAO interviewed government officials, industry representatives, other service providers, and 12 plan sponsors of varying sizes and other characteristics. GAO also conducted case studies of eight managed account providers with varying characteristics by, in part, reviewing required government filings.

Chapter 2 – Over the past 25 years, defined contribution (DC) plans—including 401(k) plans—have become the most prevalent form of employer-sponsored retirement plan in the United States. The majority of assets held in these plans are invested in stocks and stock mutual funds, and the decline in the major stock market indices in 2008 greatly reduced the value of many families' retirement savings. The effect of stock market volatility on families' retirement savings is just one issue of concern to Congress with respect to defined contribution retirement plans.

This report describes seven major policy issues with respect to defined contribution plans:

1) *Access to employer-sponsored retirement plans.* In 2007, only 61% of employees in the private sector were offered a retirement plan of any kind at work. Fifty-five percent were offered a DC plan. Only 45% of workers at establishments with fewer than 100 employees were offered a retirement plan of any kind in 2007. Forty-two percent were offered a defined contribution plan.
2) *Participation in employer-sponsored plans.* Between 20% and 25% of workers whose employer offers a DC plan do not participate. Workers under age 35 are less likely than older workers to participate.
3) *Contribution rates.* On average, participants in DC plans contributed 6% of pay to the plan in 2007. The median contribution by household heads who participated in a DC plan in 2007 was $3,360. This was just 22% of the maximum allowable contribution of $15,500 in that year.
4) *Investment choices.* At year-end 2007, 78% of all DC plan assets were invested in stocks and stock mutual funds. This ratio varied little by age, indicating that many workers nearing retirement were heavily invested in stocks and risked substantial losses in a market downturn like that in 2008. Investment education and target date funds could help workers make better investment decisions.
5) *Fee disclosure.* Retirement plans contract with service providers to provide investment management, record-keeping, and other services. There can be many service providers, each charging a fee that is ultimately paid by participants in 401(k) plans. The arrangements through which service providers are compensated can be very complicated and fees are often not clearly disclosed.
6) *Leakage from retirement savings.* Pre-retirement withdrawals from retirement accounts are sometimes called "leakages." Current law represents a compromise between limiting leakages from retirement accounts and allowing people to have access to their retirement funds in times of great need. In general, borrowing from a 401(k) plan poses less risk to retirement security than a withdrawal. Pre-retirement withdrawals can have adverse long-term effects on retirement income.
7) *Converting retirement savings into income.* Retirees face many financial risks, including living longer than they expected, investment losses, inflation, and possible large expenses for medical care and

long-term care. Annuities can protect retirees from some of these risks, but few retirees purchase them. Developing polices that motivate retirees to convert assets into a reliable source of income will be a continuing challenge for Congress and other policymakers.

Chapter 3 – As households become more reliant on 401(k) plans and other defined contribution pension plans for future retirement income, policymakers have become more concerned that participants could be unaware of the fees charged in their plans. Small differences in fees charged can have large impacts on account balances upon retirement. This report provides information on the kinds of fees that are charged in 401(k) and other defined contribution plans.

In: Managed 401(k) Accounts
Editor: Harold Parker
ISBN: 978-1-63463-592-9

Chapter 1

401(K) PLANS: IMPROVEMENTS CAN BE MADE TO BETTER PROTECT PARTICIPANTS IN MANAGED ACCOUNTS*

United States Government Accountability Office

WHY GAO DID THIS STUDY

401(k) plan sponsors have increasingly offered participants managed accounts—*services* under which providers manage participants' 401(k) savings over time by making investment and portfolio decisions for them. These services differ from investment options offered within 401(k) plans. Because little is known about whether managed accounts are advantageous for participants and whether sponsors understand their own role and potential risks, GAO was asked to review these services.

GAO examined (1) how providers structure managed accounts, (2) their advantages and disadvantages for participants, and (3) challenges sponsors face in selecting and overseeing providers. In conducting this work, GAO reviewed relevant federal laws and regulations and surveyed plan sponsors. GAO interviewed government officials, industry representatives, other service providers, and 12 plan sponsors of varying sizes and other characteristics.

* This is an edited, reformatted and augmented version of the United States Government Accountability Office publication, GAO-14-310, dated June 2014.

GAO also conducted case studies of eight managed account providers with varying characteristics by, in part, reviewing required government filings.

What GAO Recommends

Among other things, GAO recommends that DOL consider provider fiduciary roles, require disclosure of performance and benchmarking information to plan sponsors and participants, and provide guidance to help sponsors better select and oversee managed account providers. In response, DOL agreed with GAO's recommendations and will consider changes to regulations and guidance to address any issues.

What GAO Found

GAO's review of eight managed account providers who, in 2013, represented an estimated 95 percent of the industry involved in defined contribution plans, showed that they varied in how they structured managed accounts, including the services they offered and their reported fiduciary roles. Providers used varying strategies to manage participants' accounts and incorporated varying types and amounts of participant information. In addition, GAO found some variation in how providers reported their fiduciary roles. One of the eight providers GAO reviewed had a different fiduciary role than the other seven providers, which could ultimately provide less liability protection for sponsors for the consequences of the provider's choices. The Department of Labor (DOL) requires managed account providers who offer services to defaulted participants to generally have the type of fiduciary role that provides certain levels of fiduciary protection for sponsors and assurances to participants of the provider's qualifications. DOL does not have a similar explicit requirement for providers who offer services to participants on an opt-in basis. Absent explicit requirements from DOL, some providers may actively choose to structure their services to limit the fiduciary liability protection they offer.

According to providers and sponsors, participants in managed accounts receive improved diversification and experience higher savings rates compared to those not enrolled in the service; however, these advantages can be offset by paying additional fees over time. Providers charge additional fees for managed accounts that range from $8 to $100 on every $10,000 in a participant's account. As a result, some participants pay a low fee each year while others pay a comparatively large fee on their account balance. Using the limited fee and performance data available, GAO found that the potential long-term effect of managed accounts could vary significantly, sometimes resulting in managed account participants paying substantial additional fees and experiencing lower account balances over time compared to other managed account participants. Further, participants generally do not receive performance and benchmarking information for their managed accounts. Without this information, participants cannot accurately evaluate the service and make effective decisions about their retirement investments. Even though DOL has required disclosure of similar information for 401(k) plan investments, it generally does not require sponsors to provide this type of information for managed accounts.

Sponsors are challenged by insufficient guidance and inconsistent performance information when selecting and overseeing managed account providers. DOL has not issued guidance specific to managed accounts on how sponsors should select and oversee providers, as it has done for other funds. GAO found that the absence of guidance for managed accounts has led to inconsistency in sponsors' procedures for selecting and overseeing providers. Without better guidance, plan sponsors may be unable to select a provider who offers an effective service for a reasonable fee. In addition, DOL generally does not require providers to furnish sponsors with performance and benchmarking information for managed accounts, as it does for investments available in a plan, although some providers do furnish similar information. Without this information, sponsors cannot effectively compare providers when making a selection or determine whether managed accounts are positively affecting participants' retirement savings.

ABBREVIATIONS

BLS	Bureau of Labor Statistics
DOL	U.S. Department of Labor
EBRI	Employee Benefit Research Institute
EBSA	Employee Benefits Security Administration
ERISA	Employee Retirement Income Security Act of 1974
IRA	Individual Retirement Account
MVO	Mean-Variance Optimization
PPA	Pension Protection Act of 2006

QDIA	Qualified Default Investment Alternative
RIA	Registered Investment Adviser
SEC	U.S. Securities and Exchange Commission

* * *

June 25, 2014

The Honorable George Miller
Ranking Member
Committee on Education and the Workforce
House of Representatives

Many 401(k) plan participants lack the knowledge, interest, or time to manage their retirement accounts.[1] In response, plan sponsors have increasingly offered managed account services to their participants.[2] In managed accounts, service providers make investment and portfolio decisions for participants in employer-sponsored 401(k) plans.[3] Managed accounts typically provide customized investment management of participants' 401(k) accounts as they accumulate, and sometimes as they spend down, their retirement savings.

Similar investment arrangements have been offered to retail investors since the 1970s, but managed accounts have gained popularity in 401(k) plans in part due to regulations issued by the Department of Labor (DOL) in 2007 providing that certain managed accounts could be used as "qualified default investment alternatives" in 401(k) plans. We estimate that the total amount of defined contribution plan assets in managed accounts exceeded $100 billion at the end of 2012.[4] Demand for managed accounts may continue to grow, as these services may be attractive to the many 401(k) plan participants who may lack the knowledge or initiative to make prudent choices about how much to contribute and how to direct their assets among investment options in their plan.

However, the increasing trend to offer managed accounts in 401(k) plans has raised some concerns about whether such services are advantageous for participants in terms of service and cost and whether sponsors understand their role in overseeing the use of managed accounts. In light of these concerns, you asked us to examine managed accounts in 401(k) plans.

In conducting this work, we answered the following questions:

1) How do service providers structure managed accounts?
2) What are the advantages and disadvantages of managed accounts for 401(k) plan participants?
3) What challenges, if any, do plan sponsors face in selecting and overseeing managed account providers?

To answer these questions, we reviewed relevant research and federal laws, regulations, and guidance on managed accounts in 401(k) plans.[5] To examine the key issues related to managed accounts in 401(k) plans and gather data about their prevalence and performance, we conducted in-depth case studies of eight selected managed account providers that, according to our estimates, represented over 95 percent of the managed account industry in defined contribution plans, as measured by assets under management in 2013. We selected providers based on their size, location, and legal and fee structures. We also interviewed industry representatives—including academics, industry research firms, and participant advocacy groups—and government officials, including officials from DOL's Employee Benefits Security Administration (EBSA). To gain additional information on the structure of managed accounts in 401(k) plans and the role of service providers, we reviewed Securities and Exchange Commission (SEC) filings[6] for the eight managed account providers in our case studies and 22 other providers we identified during the course of our work. As part of our case studies, we reviewed available documentation on the structure of managed accounts. To further understand the different methodologies and structures of managed accounts, we developed and submitted participant scenarios to the eight providers and asked them to provide hypothetical asset allocations for those participants, which seven of them completed and returned to us. To identify the advantages and disadvantages of managed accounts for 401(k) plan participants and any challenges sponsors face in selecting and overseeing managed account providers, we reviewed relevant documentation such as quarterly managed account reports to plan sponsors and conducted semi-structured interviews with 12 plan sponsors. To identify sponsors for interviews, we conducted a non-generalizable survey facilitated through PLANSPONSOR.[7] Based on their responses to the survey, we selected sponsors with a variety of characteristics, such as plan size and managed account provider. Further, we used publicly available data to develop illustrations of how various factors may affect the outcomes of participants in managed accounts. To assess the reliability of these data, we considered the reliability and familiarity of the source of the data or information and, when necessary, interviewed representatives of those sources about their methods, internal controls, and results. We found these data sufficiently reliable for our purposes. For more information on the data and other methodologies we used see appendix I.

We conducted this performance audit from October 2012 to June 2014 in accordance with generally accepted government auditing standards. Those standards require that we plan and perform the audit to obtain sufficient, appropriate evidence to provide a reasonable basis for our findings and conclusions based on our audit objectives. We believe that the evidence obtained provides a reasonable basis for our findings and conclusions based on our audit objectives.

BACKGROUND

Under Title I of the Employee Retirement Income Security Act of 1974 (ERISA), as amended, employers are permitted to sponsor defined contribution plans in which an employee's retirement savings are based on contributions and the performance of the investments in individual accounts. Typically, 401(k) plans—the predominant type of defined contribution plan in the United States—allow employees who participate in the plan to specify the size of their contributions and direct their assets to one or more investments among the options offered within the plan.[8] Investment options generally include mutual funds, stable value funds,[9] company stock, and money market funds. To help participants make optimal investment choices, an increasing number of plans are offering professionally managed allocations—including managed accounts—in their 401(k) plan lineups.

Managed accounts are *investment services* under which providers make investment decisions for specific participants to allocate their retirement savings among a mix of assets they have determined to be appropriate for the participant based on their personal information. As shown in figure 1, managed accounts were first offered to 401(k) plans around 1990, but most providers did not start offering them until after 2000.

Managed accounts differ from other professionally managed allocations, such as target date funds and balanced funds, in several key ways. Target date funds (also known as life cycle funds) are *products* that determine an asset allocation that would be appropriate for a participant of a certain age or retirement date and adjust that allocation so it becomes more conservative as the fund approaches its intended target date.[10] Target date funds do not place participants into an asset allocation; instead, participants generally self-select into a target date fund they feel is appropriate for them based on the fund's predetermined glide path that governs asset allocation. Balanced funds are *products* that generally invest in a fixed mix of assets (e.g., 60 percent equity and 40 percent fixed income assets). While target date funds manage the fund to reach a target date, managed accounts may consider other, more personalized factors such as a participant's stated risk tolerance,[11] even though they are not required to do so. As shown in figure 2, managed accounts may offer higher levels of personalization than other types of professionally managed allocations.

Managed Accounts in Other Workplace Defined Contribution Plans and Individual Retirement Accounts (IRAs)

As managed accounts have gained popularity in 401(k) plans, there are indications that they may also be gaining popularity in government and non-profit workplace retirement savings plans, commonly referred to as 457 or 403(b) plans. Many of the providers we spoke to that offer managed accounts to 401(k) plans also offer services to other plans like these. In addition, some providers are starting to offer managed accounts in IRAs, and in particular rollover IRAs—when participants separate from their employer they may decide to roll their funds into an IRA. One of these providers noted that it is easier to engage participants who use managed accounts through products such as IRAs, and there is more flexibility with investment options, even though the provider's marketing costs may be higher.

Source: GAO analysis of provider information | GAO-14-310.

Managed accounts are generally considered to be an investment service—not one of the plan's investment options—while target date funds are considered to be investment options. In the latter, participants can invest all or a portion of their 401(k) plan contributions in a target date fund, but generally cannot directly invest in a managed account. Instead, the role of the participant is to enroll in the managed account service, or be defaulted into it, generally relinquishing their ability to make investment decisions unless they disenroll from, or opt out of, the managed account. As shown in figure 3, managed account providers decide how to invest contributions, generally among the investment options available in a 401(k) plan, and then manage these investments over time to help participants reach their retirement savings goals. By comparison, participants not enrolled in a managed account have to make their own decisions about how to invest their 401(k) plan contributions.

DOL Oversight

DOL's Employee Benefits Security Administration (EBSA) is the primary agency through which Title I of ERISA is enforced to protect private pension plan participants and beneficiaries from the misuse or theft of their pension assets. To carry out its responsibilities, EBSA issues regulations and guidance; investigates plan sponsors,[12] fiduciaries, and service providers; seeks appropriate remedies to correct violations of the law; and pursues litigation when it deems necessary. As part of its mission, DOL is also responsible for assisting and educating plan sponsors to help ensure the retirement security of workers and their families.

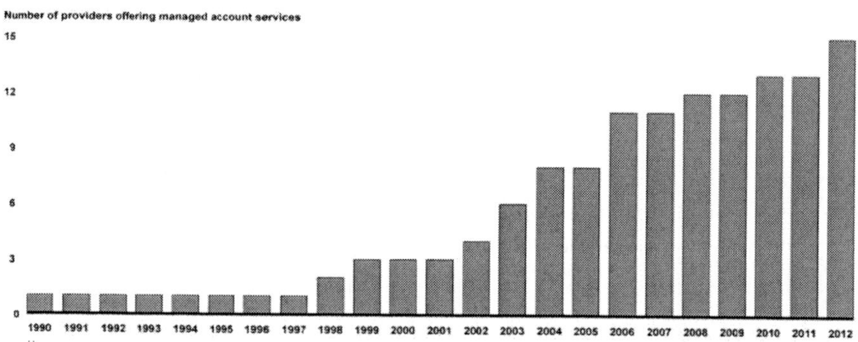

Source : GAO analysis of information from managed account providers. | GAO-14-310.

Note: This figure represents only those providers that developed the underlying discretionary management method for managing participants' accounts. Plan record keepers—providers that maintain records of participant contributions and returns—have a role in offering managed accounts to participants, but generally rely on managed account providers to develop asset allocation strategies for participant accounts. Some of these managed account providers offer their services through multiple record keepers and may be sub-contractors to record keepers. In the latter situation, the record keeper may brand the managed account as their own, but decisions about how to allocate participant retirement savings come from the managed account provider. For example, one of the managed account providers listed in this figure provides its discretionary managed account services through 18 record keepers. Thus, participants in plans that use one of those 18 record keepers may all receive the same underlying discretionary management, but their record keeper may brand the managed account differently.

Figure 1. Number of Managed Account Providers Serving 401(k) Plans Since 1990.

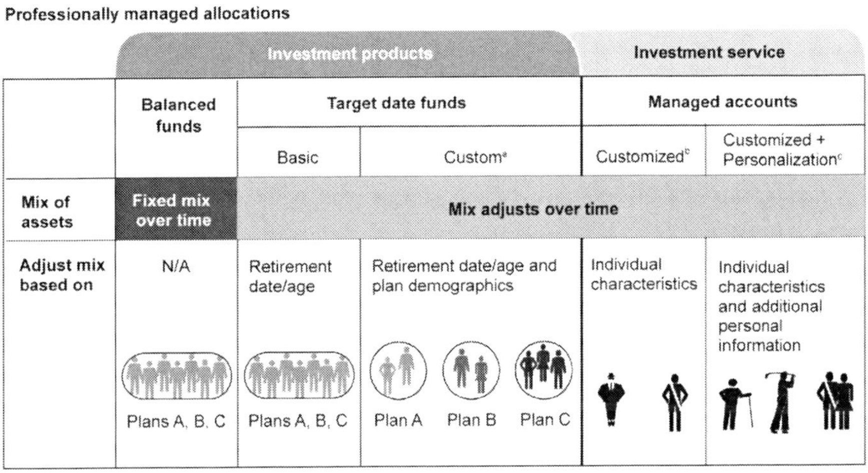

Source: GAO analysis of DOL publications, industry publications, and information from plan sponsors, record keepers, and managed account providers. | GAO-14-310.

[a] Some plan sponsors have established custom target date funds instead of relying on preexisting target date funds offered by investment management firms. Custom target date funds can be more precisely tailored to match a plan's objectives and demographics, and offer a plan sponsor greater control over the underlying investments of a target date fund. However, custom target date funds may involve costs greater than those of an already-existing fund, so they may be more popular among larger plan sponsors.

[b] In customized managed account services, the provider allocates a participant's account based solely on the participant's age or based on additional factors that can be easily obtained from the plan's record keeper, such as gender, income, current account balance, and current savings rate.

[c] Personalization by managed account providers includes not only a review of age and recordkeeping data, but the provider also allows participants to provide personalized information such as stating their preferences for risk or the availability of spousal assets to inform the asset allocation process.

Figure 2. Key Differences among Balanced Funds, Target Date Funds, and Managed Accounts in 401(k) Plans.

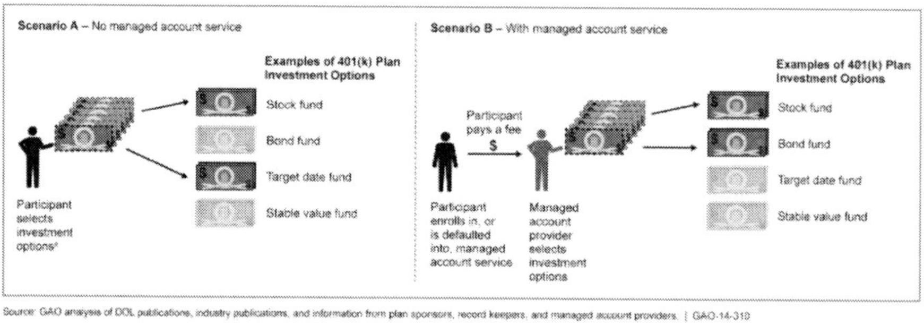

Source: GAO analysis of DOL publications, industry publications, and information from plan sponsors, record keepers, and managed account providers. | GAO-14-310.

[a] When sponsors do not offer managed account services, they may decide to default participants into an investment option such as a target date fund.

Figure 3. Example of How Managed Account Providers Make Investment Decisions For Participants.

Managed Accounts as Qualified Default Investment Alternatives and Opt-in Services

In 2007, DOL designated certain managed accounts as one type of investment that may be eligible as a qualified default investment alternative (QDIA) into which 401(k) plan fiduciaries may default participants who do not provide investment directions with respect to their plan contributions.[13] DOL designated three categories of investments that may be eligible as QDIAs if all requirements of the QDIA regulation have been satisfied—these categories generally include: (1) an investment product or model portfolio that is designed to become more conservative as the participant's age increases (e.g., a target date or lifecycle fund); (2) an investment product or model portfolio that is designed with a mix of equity and fixed income exposures appropriate for the participants of the plan as a whole (e.g., a balanced fund); and (3) an investment management service that uses investment alternatives available in the plan and is designed to become more conservative as the participant's age increases (e.g., a managed account).[14] DOL regulations indicate that plan fiduciaries who comply with the QDIA regulation will not be liable for any loss to participants that occurs as a result of the investment of their assets in a QDIA, including investments made through managed account arrangements that satisfy the conditions of the QDIA regulation.[15] However, plan fiduciaries remain responsible for the prudent selection and monitoring of any QDIA offered by the plan.[16] To obtain relief, plan fiduciaries must provide participants with advance notice of the circumstances under which plan contributions or other assets will be invested on their behalf in a QDIA; a description of the QDIA's investment objectives, risk and return characteristics, and fees and expenses; and the right of participants to opt out of the QDIA, among other things.[17] A 2012 survey of defined contribution plan sponsors by PLANSPONSOR indicated that managed accounts were used as a QDIA less than 5 percent of the time.[18]

Managed accounts are also offered as opt-in services by over 30 percent of defined contribution plan sponsors. Managed accounts can be offered as both QDIA and opt-in services, allowing the plan sponsor to choose which services to offer their participants. Plan fiduciaries who offer managed account services only to participants who affirmatively elect to use the service (i.e., on an opt-in basis), rather than by default, are not required to comply with the QDIA regulation, although such fiduciaries still are subject to the general fiduciary obligations under ERISA with respect to the selection and monitoring of a managed account service for their plan.

Disclosure Regulations

Plan sponsors, including those who offer managed account services in their 401(k) plans, are required to issue a variety of informational disclosures and notices to plan participants and beneficiaries at enrollment, on a quarterly and annual basis, and when certain triggering events occur.[19] These disclosures—often referred to as participant-level disclosures—when made in accordance with regulatory requirements, help ensure that plan participants have access to the information they need to make informed decisions about their retirement investments. In addition, when a plan sponsor chooses to default participants into managed accounts as a QDIA, the sponsor must inform participants of this decision annually through a number of specific disclosures, based on the plan's design. The QDIA disclosures, when made in accordance with regulatory requirements, provide relief from certain fiduciary responsibilities for sponsors of 401(k) plans.[20]

Service providers that provide managed account services to a plan may be required to provide certain disclosures about the compensation they will receive to plan sponsors offering a managed account service under different DOL disclosure requirements. These disclosures—often referred to as service provider disclosures—are intended to provide information sufficient for sponsors to make informed decisions when selecting and monitoring service providers for their plans. DOL's final rule on these disclosures requires service providers to furnish sponsors with information to help them assess the reasonableness of total compensation paid to providers, to identify potential conflicts of interest, and to satisfy other reporting and disclosure requirements under Title I of ERISA, including the regulation governing sponsor's disclosure to participants.[21]

Roles and Fiduciary Obligations Under ERISA

Managed account provider roles may differ from those of other plan service providers. As shown in figure 4, when a plan sponsor decides to offer participants a managed account service, other entities may contribute to its implementation and operation.

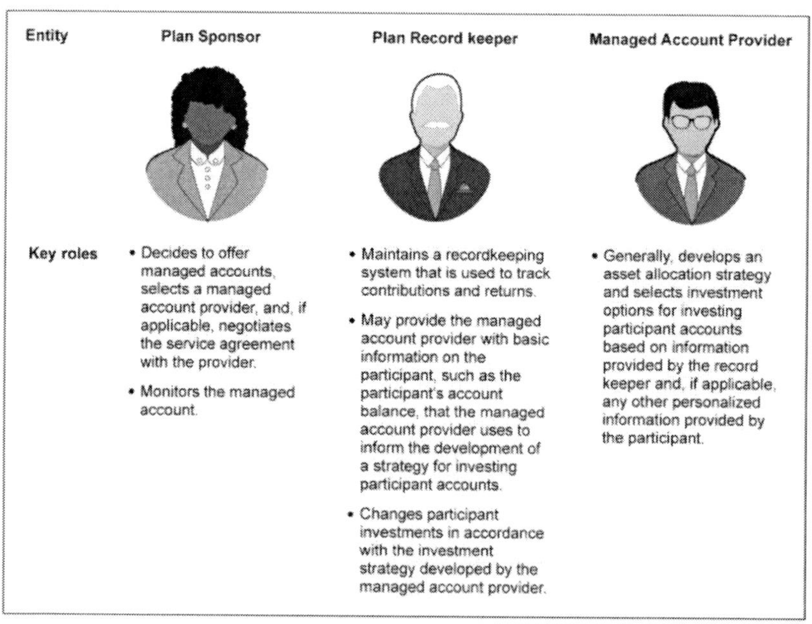

Source: GAO analysis of DOL publications, industry publications, and information from plan sponsors, record keepers, and managed account providers. | GAO-14-310.

Figure 4. Entities that May Participate in a Managed Account Service Arrangement in 401(k) Plans.

Some record keepers and intermediary[22] service providers refer to themselves as "managed account providers" because they make this service available to participants, but they do not ultimately decide how to invest participant contributions.[23] Similarly, even though target date fund managers or collective investment trust managers may select an overall asset allocation strategy and investments to fit that strategy for the funds they offer to 401(k) plan participants, these managers also do not ultimately decide how to invest participant accounts.[24]

Plan sponsors are typically the named fiduciaries of the plan. Managed account providers and record keepers may also be fiduciaries, depending on their roles and the services they provide. Fiduciaries are required to carry out their responsibilities prudently and solely in the interest of the plan's participants and beneficiaries.[25] Plan service providers that have investment discretion or provide investment advice about how to invest participant accounts generally may be "3(38) Investment Manager" fiduciaries or "3(21) Investment Adviser" fiduciaries.[26] A 3(38) Investment Manager fiduciary can only be a bank, an insurance company, or a Registered Investment Adviser (RIA). Under ERISA, 3(38) Investment Manager fiduciaries have the power to manage, acquire, or dispose of plan assets, and they acknowledge, in writing, that they are a fiduciary with respect to the plan. In contrast, a 3(21) Investment Adviser fiduciary usually does not have authority to manage, acquire, or dispose of plan assets, but is still a fiduciary because its investment recommendations may exercise some level of influence and control over the investments made by the plan. When managed account services are offered as QDIAs, the managed account provider is generally required to be a 3(38) Investment Manager fiduciary. There is no similar explicit requirement for managed account providers whose services are offered within a plan on an opt-in basis.[27]

Providers Structure Managed Accounts Differently, which Can Harm Participants

Managed Account Providers Vary Their Services

Managed account providers vary how they provide services, even though they generally offer the same basic service—initial and ongoing investment management of a 401(k) plan participant's account based on generally accepted industry methods. The eight providers in our case studies use different investment options, employ varying strategies to develop and adjust asset allocations for participants, incorporate varying types and amounts of participant information, and rebalance participant accounts at different intervals.[28] As a result, participants with similar characteristics in different plans may have differing experiences.

Investment Options

To develop participant asset allocations, most of the eight providers in our case studies use the investment options chosen by the plan sponsor.[29] By contrast, other providers require plan sponsors that want to offer their managed account to accept a preselected list of investment options from which the provider will determine participant asset allocations, including exchange traded funds[30] or asset classes not typically found in 401(k) plan lineups, such as commodities. Because they are atypical investment options, participants who do not sign up for managed accounts may not be able to access them. Compared to typical 401(k) plan investment options, these atypical investment options may provide broader exposure to certain markets and opportunities to diversify participant retirement assets.

Asset Allocation Strategies

The eight managed account providers in our case studies generally reported making asset allocation decisions based on modern portfolio theory, which sets a goal of taking enough risk so that participants' 401(k) account balances may earn large enough returns over time to meet their retirement savings goals, but not so much that their balances could earn lower or even negative returns.[31] Managed account providers generally help participants by constructing portfolios that attempt to provide maximum expected returns with a given level of risk, but their strategies can range from formal to informal. The formal way of determining this type of portfolio is called "mean-variance optimization" (MVO), under which providers plot risk and return characteristics of all combinations of investment options in the plan and choose the portfolio that maximizes expected return for a given level of risk.[32] There are a number of specific techniques that managed account providers can apply to improve the quality and sophistication of asset allocations, including Monte Carlo simulation.[33] However, some providers incorporated less formal ways of achieving a diversified portfolio, such as active management and experience-based methods.[34] The eight providers in our case studies use varying strategies and participant goals to develop and adjust asset allocations for participants, as shown in table 1. As a result, participants with similar characteristics may end up with different asset allocations.

Providers' use of different asset allocation strategies leads to variation in the asset allocations participants actually experience. As shown in figure 5, four of the eight providers in our case studies vary in their recommendations of specific investment options for a 30-year old participant.[35]

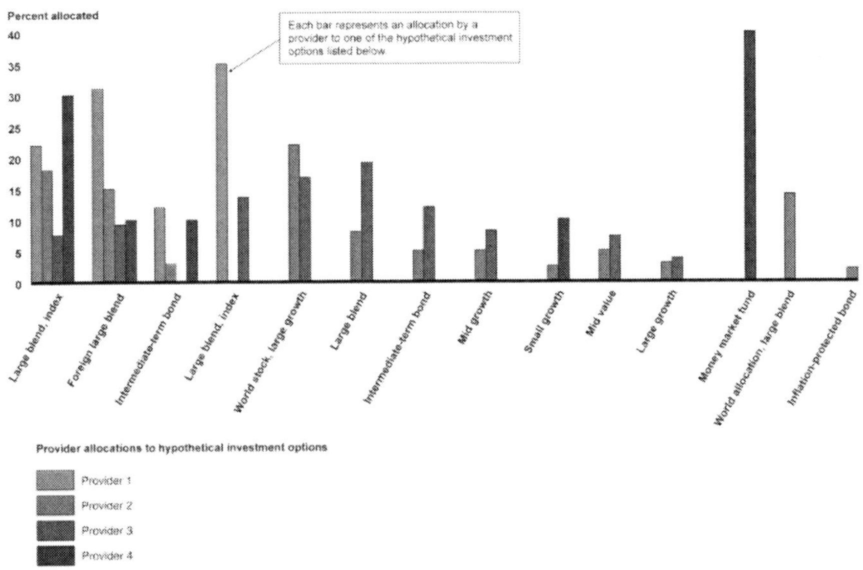

Source: GAO analysis o provider asset allocations. | GAO-14-130.

Note: This figure presents illustrative allocations from four case study providers for our hypothetical 30-year-old participant. Investment option categories presented here are based on publicly reported Morningstar Fund information in January 2014 for the 14 mutual funds that we selected for hypothetical plan investment options based on available information about whether these funds could be found in 401(k) plans.

Figure 5. Selected Provider Allocations to Hypothetical Investment Options for a Hypothetical 30-year-old Participant.

Table 1. Eight Providers' Strategies for Developing 401(k) Managed Account Participant Asset Allocations

Provider	Strategies	Participant goal (percent of participant's final ending compensation)[a]	Description
A	Mean-variance optimization (MVO),[b] Monte Carlo,[c] and experience-based[d]	100 percent	According to this provider, it has 19 options for the equity percentage of the participant's account, and 31 options for years to retirement. This provider builds an efficient frontier for asset classes, but also considers lifecycle theory, evaluating changing participant risk tolerances over time and tradeoffs between a participant's financial and human capital.
B	MVO	85 percent	According to this provider, it constructs 101 portfolios per plan—one for each equity/fixed income combination. If a participant is defaulted into the managed account or does not provide personalized information, this provider will determine the participant's asset allocation solely on their investment time horizon. If the participant provides personalized information, this provider will assess their personal financial situation to determine an appropriate asset allocation. Based on this asset allocation, this provider places the participant into the appropriate portfolio.
C	MVO, Monte Carlo, and experience-based	80 percent or higher	According to this provider, it creates 10 asset allocation model portfolios using the investment options in the plan and places participants in 1 of the 10 model portfolios based on their risk profile. It uses a glide path approach to reduce risk in each portfolio over time.[e] This provider noted that it believes its glide path approach is more conservative than many target date fund glide paths.
D	MVO, Monte Carlo, and experience-based	80 percent	This provider said it tends to be more conservative, investing participants' 401(k) account balances more heavily in fixed income assets and setting parameters for international and emerging market

Provider	Strategies	Participant goal (percent of participant's final ending compensation)[a]	Description
			assets, to increase the probability that participants will achieve their retirement savings goals.
E	MVO and experience- based	70 percent	According to this provider, it allocates participant accounts to 1 of 50 steps on one of three glide paths based on the participant's age and ratio of retirement assets to liabilities. This provider uses actuarial calculations to determine participant "funded ratios"—dividing the total amount of money the participant is expected to have saved at retirement by the total amount of money the participant needs to have saved in order to fund lifetime retirement income.
F	MVO, Monte Carlo, and experience-based	70 percent	According to this provider, it creates individualized strategies for each participant, which this provider noted results in unique portfolios for approximately 80 percent of its participant population. Unlike other providers, it does not set asset allocation targets prior to selecting investment options.
G	Active management[f]	No goal specified	This provider said it develops a set of five portfolios using exchange traded funds.[g] Each portfolio has a dedicated flexible portion for which the provider will be able to adjust between equity assets and cash based on market conditions. This provider places participants in one of the portfolios based on their age.
H	Experience-based	No goal specified	This provider said it generally relies on a time horizon based formula to determine optimal asset allocations for participants. This provider's default formula is to subtract the participant's age from 100 and allocate that percent of the participant's account to an equity pool of assets, with the remainder allocated to a fixed income pool.[h] This provider includes in the fixed income pool estimates of the total value a participant could expect to receive from defined benefit plans and Social Security retirement benefits.

Source: GAO analysis of information provided by managed account providers. | GAO-14-310.

[a] Managed account providers have different philosophies about how much a participant should expect to spend during retirement, generally communicated as a percentage of the participant's expected final ending compensation. The goal they determine for participants may be an integral part of the provider's strategy for determining the participant's appropriate asset allocation. Providers that calculate this goal may provide participants status updates on their progress towards achieving this goal.

[b] MVO is the formal way of constructing portfolios that balance risk and return. It entails plotting risk and return characteristics of all combinations of investment options in the plan and choosing the portfolio that maximizes expected return for a given level of risk.

[c] Monte Carlo simulation describes the range of outcomes from a given asset allocation assuming various inputs for expected returns, volatilities, and correlations of investment options in the plan.

[d] Experience-based methods for developing asset allocations rely on tradition, experience, or rules of thumb and may be less expensive to implement than MVO strategies. Popular experience-based methods could include allocation to fixed income assets increase with participants' risk aversion or allocation to equity assets remain at one hundred minus the participant's age.

[e] A "glide path" approach generally adjusts participant risk levels downward over time.

[f] Active management strategies seek to achieve specific goals and require more hands-on management of the fund by the investment manager than passively managed funds. This provider uses a rules-based approach, but also considers market trends in actively managing the flexible portion of their asset allocation.

[g] Exchange traded funds are similar to mutual funds in that they offer investors a way to pool their money in a fund that makes investments in stocks, bonds, or other assets and, in return, to receive an interest in an investment pool. However, shares of the exchange traded funds are traded on a national stock exchange and at market prices that may or may not be the same as the net asset value of the shares. Unlike traditional mutual funds, exchange traded funds do not sell individual shares directly to investors, and investors may not redeem individual shares; the funds only issue and redeem their shares in large blocks known as creation units.

[h] While one hundred minus age is this provider's default method for determining asset allocation to equities, the provider noted that plan sponsors may specify other methods of determining the appropriate asset allocation to equity assets.

Type and Amount of Participant Information

The type and amount of information providers use can also affect the way participant account balances are allocated. For example, two of the eight providers in our case studies only offer a *customized* service—allocating a participant's account based solely on age or other factors that can be easily obtained from the plan's record keeper, such as gender, income, current account balance, and current savings rate. The other six providers also offer a *personalized* service that takes into account additional personal information to inform asset allocations, such as risk tolerance or spousal assets. Providers that offer a personalized service reported that personalization could lead to better asset allocation for participants, but they also reported that generally fewer than one-third, and sometimes fewer than 15 percent, of participants furnish this personalized information. As a result, some industry representatives felt that participants may not be getting the full value of the service for which they are paying. For example, participants who are defaulted into managed accounts that offer a highly personalized service run the risk of paying for services they are not using if they are disengaged from their retirement investments. As shown in table 2, we found that among five of the seven providers that furnished asset allocations for our hypothetical scenarios, there was little relationship between the level of personalization and the fee they charged to participants for the managed account service.[36]

Some managed account providers' services may become more beneficial as participants age or as their situations become more complex because personalization seeks to create a tailored asset allocation for each participant. Such an individualized approach could even mean that older participants who are close to retirement and very young participants just starting their careers could be placed in equally risky allocations based on their personalized circumstances. However, industry representatives told us that participants who never supply additional, personalized information to managed account providers may be allocated similarly over time to those participants in target date funds.

Table 2. Effect on Provider Allocations Using Personalized Information for 30- and 57-year-old Hypothetical Participants

Provider	Effect of adding participants' personalized information on the asset allocation of a hypothetical 30-year-old participant[a]	Effect of adding participants' personalized information on the asset allocation of a hypothetical 57-year-old participant[a]	Comparative size of additional managed account fee charged to participants (range from 0.08 to 1 percent)[b]
A	Change	Change	Middle
B	Change	Change	Higher
C	No change	Change	Lower
D	No change	Change	Lower to higher
E	Nearly the same[c]	No change	Lower
F	No change	No change	Lowest to middle
G	No change	No change	Middle

Source: GAO analysis of provider asset allocations. | GAO-14-310.

Note: Seven of the eight providers in our case studies submitted example asset allocations for five hypothetical participant scenarios in one hypothetical plan. Two of the five hypothetical participant scenarios pertain to a 30-year old participant and another two pertain to a hypothetical 57-year old participant. For each hypothetical participant, one scenario only included customized information—age or other factors that can be easily obtained from the plan's record keeper, such as gender, income, current account balance, and current savings rate—and the other scenario provided the same customized information but with additional, personal information, such as the hypothetical participant's preference for risk or their spouse's assets.

[a] We compared the asset allocations sent by the seven providers for the 30-year old and 57-year old participants to determine how the additional, personal information affected their hypothetical asset allocations and report here whether the asset allocations for each provider changed, were nearly the same, or did not change. Providers A through E in this table told us that additional personal information affects their asset allocations, which was generally confirmed by the differences in their asset allocations. For example, provider A's mid-range fee is less than could be expected given that personalization resulted in different asset allocations for both

participants, while provider E's low fee is to be expected given that personalization generally did not result in different asset allocations for either participant. In contrast, providers F and G told us that they only offer a customized service, which was confirmed by the fact that their asset allocations did not change for each hypothetical participant.

[b] Providers in our case studies told us the range of fees they typically charge participants who use their services—generally between 0.08 and 1 percent of the value of the assets providers manage for the participant. Here, we have included a comparative statement about the fee that participants could be charged if they enrolled in, or were defaulted into, managed accounts with one of these providers.

[c] We categorized this provider's asset allocations as "nearly the same" because they differed by less than 5 percent. Comparatively, allocations classified as the "No change" were exactly the same, and allocations classified as "Change" differed by more than 10 percent and sometimes by over 300 percent.

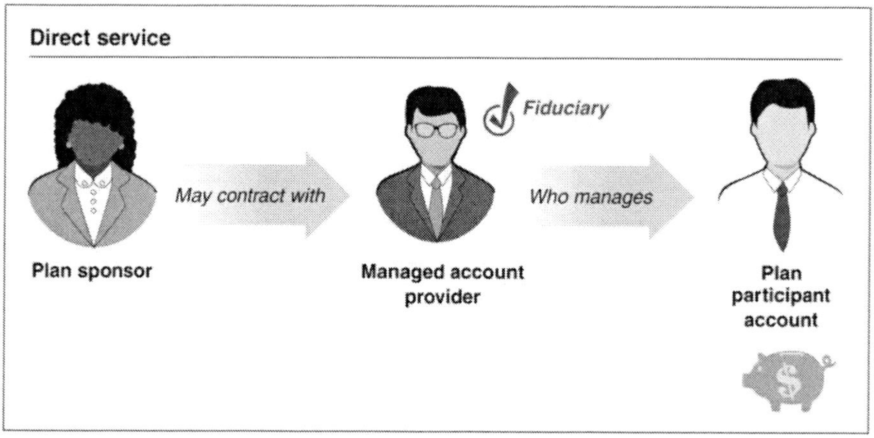

Source: GAO analysis of managed account provider case studies. | GAO-14-130.

Note: Plan sponsors are typically the named fiduciaries of the plan. In addition, all eight managed account providers included in our case studies told us they take on some level of fiduciary responsibility for the managed account, regardless of whether their services are offered as a Qualified Default Investment Alternative or on an opt-in basis.

Figure 6. Example of a Direct Managed Account Arrangement in a 401(k) Plan.

Rebalancing Approaches and Time Frames

Providers differ in their approaches and time frames for rebalancing participant managed accounts—adjusting participant accounts to reflect any changes to their asset allocation strategies based on changing market conditions and participant information. Seven of the eight providers in our case studies use a "glide path" approach to systematically reduce participant risk over time but one does not set predetermined glide paths for participants. Similarly, two of the eight providers in our case studies rebalance participant accounts annually, while the other providers generally review and rebalance participant accounts at least quarterly. Despite these differences in approaches and timeframes, our analysis of provider hypothetical asset allocations indicated that providers generally allocated less to equity assets and more to fixed income or cash-like assets for the older hypothetical participants than for the younger hypothetical participant.[37]

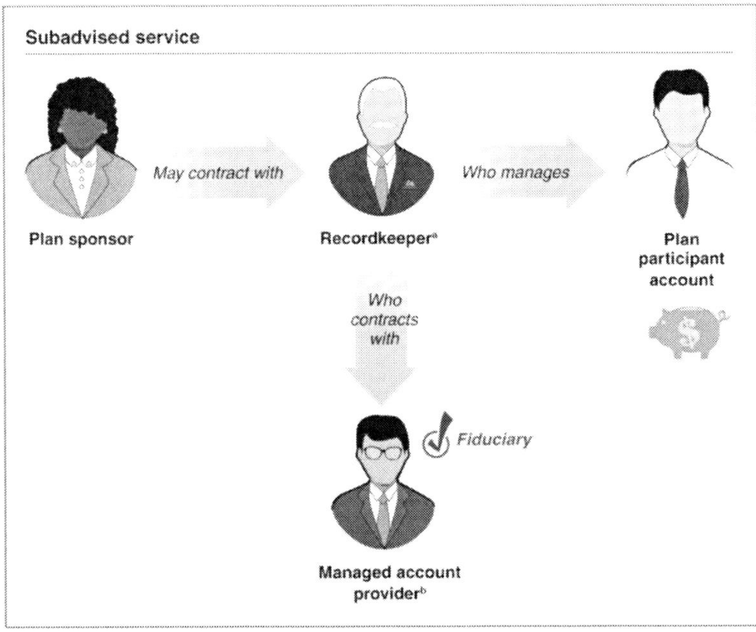

Source: GAO analysis of managed account provider case studies. | GAO-14-310.

Note: Plan sponsors are typically the named fiduciaries of the plan. In addition, all eight managed account providers included in our case studies told us they take on some level of fiduciary responsibility for the managed account, regardless of whether their services are offered as a Qualified Default Investment Alternative or on an opt-in basis. Subadvised arrangements can be offered in multiple ways. For example, providers can charge level fees or could follow the structure laid out in the Department of Labor's SunAmerica Advisory Opinion 2001-09A (December 2001).

[a] Record keepers or their affiliates may also take on fiduciary roles, depending on the services they provide.

[b] When a record keeper contracts with an intermediary provider that offers the use of multiple managed account providers, the intermediary would take the place of the managed account provider in this graphic and the multiple managed account providers that contract with the intermediary would be below the intermediary.

Figure 7. Example of a Subadvised Managed Account Arrangement in a 401(k) Plan.

Providers Vary Their Fiduciary Roles and Some May Offer Less Liability Protection for Sponsors

Some managed account providers in our case studies offer their services under "direct" arrangements in which the plan sponsor directly contracts with a provider to offer these services, as shown in figure 6.[38] According to the providers we spoke with, managed account providers in this type of arrangement are generally fiduciaries, but record keepers may not be fiduciaries with respect to the managed account service, as their role consists primarily of providing information to the managed account provider and implementing asset allocation changes to participant accounts.[39]

By contrast, some managed account providers use "subadvised" arrangements to offer their services. According to the providers we spoke to, in these arrangements, the plan sponsor does not directly contract with the managed account provider, and the plan's record keeper, or an affiliate, may take on some fiduciary responsibility with respect to the managed account, as shown in figure 7. The record keeper may fulfill some of the responsibilities the managed account provider would have in a direct arrangement. These responsibilities may include providing periodic rebalancing based on the provider's strategy, marketing managed account services, or offering other ongoing support for participants.[40]

All of the eight managed account providers in our case studies told us that they take on some level of fiduciary responsibility—regardless of whether their services are offered as QDIAs or on an opt-in basis—so they each offer some protections to sponsors and participants in managed accounts. Seven of the providers in our case studies told us that they willingly accept 3(38) Investment Manager fiduciary status for discretionary management over participant accounts,[41] but one of the eight providers in our case studies noted that it never accepts 3(38) Investment Manager fiduciary status because it only has discretion over participants' accounts once a year.[42] This provider told us that it is only a 3(21) Investment Adviser fiduciary even though its managed account service is similar to that of the other providers in our case studies.[43] Under ERISA, 3(21) Investment Adviser fiduciaries usually do not have authority over plan assets, but they may influence the operation of the plan by providing advice to sponsors and participants for a fee.[44] As such, they are generally liable for the consequences when their advice is imprudent or disloyal. In contrast, a 3(38) Investment Manager fiduciary has authority to manage plan assets at their discretion and with prudent judgment, and is also liable for the consequences of imprudent or disloyal decisions. Because 3(38)

Investment Manager fiduciaries have explicit discretionary authority and must have the qualifications of a bank, insurance company, or RIA,[45] sponsors who use 3(38) Investment Manager fiduciaries may receive a broader level of liability protection from those providers as opposed to providers who offer managed account services as 3(21) Investment Adviser fiduciaries.[46] In addition, when a 3(38) Investment Manager fiduciary is used, participants may have a broader level of assurance that they are receiving services from a qualified manager in light of the requirements related to qualifications of such fiduciaries.

As noted previously, when managed account services are offered as QDIAs, DOL requires the managed account provider to generally be a 3(38) Investment Manager fiduciary, but DOL has no similar explicit requirement for managed account providers whose services are offered on an opt-in basis.[47] Absent explicit requirements or additional guidance from DOL, some managed account providers may choose to structure the services they provide to limit their fiduciary liability, which could ultimately provide less liability protection for sponsors for the consequences of provider investment management choices. Given the current lack of direction or guidance about appropriate fiduciary roles for providers that offer managed accounts on an opt-in basis, sponsors may not be aware of this potential concern. Industry representatives we spoke with expressed concern about managed account providers who do not accept full responsibility with respect to managed account services by acknowledging their role as a 3(38) Investment Manager fiduciary. Other representatives also noted that it was important for sponsors to understand providers' fiduciary responsibilities given the important differences between 3(21) Investment Adviser and 3(38) Investment Manager fiduciaries with respect to the nature of liability protection they may provide for sponsors and the services they may provide for both sponsors and participants.

Some Providers Offer Additional Services That Could Lead to Conflicts of Interest, which DOL Has Not Addressed

Managed account providers may offer potentially valuable additional services to participants in or near retirement regarding how to spend down their accumulated retirement savings, but these services could lead to potential conflicts of interest. Most of the providers in our case studies allow participants to continue receiving account management services when they retire as long as they leave all or a portion of their retirement savings in the 401(k) plan. Some of those providers also provide potentially useful additional services to participants in or near retirement and do not typically charge additional fees for doing so.[48] These services may include helping participants review the tax consequences of withdrawals from their 401(k) account and advising them about when and how to claim Social Security retirement benefits. However, these providers may have a financial disincentive to recommend an out-of-plan option, such as an annuity or rollover to other plans or IRAs, because it is advantageous for them to have participants' continued enrollment in their managed account service offered through a 401(k) plan.

Providers have developed ways to mitigate some of this potential conflict of interest by, for example, offering advice on alternate sources of income in retirement such as TIPS.[49] Regardless, representatives from a participant advocacy group noted that managed account providers should have little involvement in a participant's decision about whether to stay in the managed account. As part of its responsibilities to protect plan participants under ERISA, DOL has not specifically addressed whether conflicts of interest may exist with respect to managed accounts offering additional services to participants in or near retirement.[50] As a result, participants can be easily persuaded to stay in the managed account given the additional services offered to them by managed account providers.[51] Additionally, the ease that these services offer could discourage managed account participants from fully considering other options, which can ultimately put them at risk of making suboptimal spend-down decisions.

Managed Accounts Offer Advantages for Some Participants, But Fees and Lack of Standardized Reporting Requirements from DOL Can Offset These Advantages

Various Industry Representatives Report that Managed Accounts Can Provide a Number of Advantages for Participants

Increase Diversification

Some managed account providers and plan sponsors have said that increased diversification of retirement portfolios is the main advantage of the managed account service for 401(k) plan participants. Increased diversification for participants enrolled in a managed account can result in better risk management and increased retirement income compared to those who self-direct their 401(k) investments. For example, one provider's study of managed account performance found that the portfolios of all managed account participants were believed to have been appropriately allocated, but that 43 percent of those who self-directed their 401(k) investments had equity allocations that were believed to be inappropriate for their age, and nearly half of these participants' portfolios were improperly diversified.[52] The advantages of a diversified portfolio include reducing a participant's risk of loss, reducing volatility within the participant's account, and generating long-term positive retirement outcomes.[53]

Another reported advantage of managed accounts is that they help to moderate volatility in 401(k) account performance, compared to accounts of those who self-direct their 401(k) investments. For example, in two recent reports on managed account performance, one record keeper concluded that the expanded use of professionally managed allocations, including managed accounts, is contributing to a reduction in extreme risk and return outcomes for participants, and is also gradually mitigating concerns about the quality of portfolio decision-making within defined contribution plans.[54] Managed account providers in our eight case studies also claim that the increased personalization and more frequent rebalancing of managed accounts create an appropriately diversified portfolio that better meets a participant's retirement goals than target date funds or balanced funds. According to these providers, periodic rebalancing combats participant inertia, one of the main problems with a self-directed 401(k) account, and the failure to update investment strategies when financial circumstances change over time.[55]

Encourage Larger Contributions

Several managed account providers told us that another advantage of managed accounts is the tendency for participants to save more for retirement compared to those who are not enrolled in the service. For example, in a study of managed accounts, a provider reported that participants in plans for which this provider offers the service contributed $2,070 more on average in 2012 than participants who self-directed investments in their 401(k) accounts (1.9 percent of salary more in contributions on average than participants who self-direct 401(k) investments).[56] This provider noted that managed account participants are better at taking advantage of their plan's matching contribution than participants who self-direct their 401(k) investments. For example, they found that 69 percent of managed account participants contributed at least to the level of the maximum employer matching contribution, while only 62 percent of participants who self-directed investments contributed to this level. This provider said that communication with managed account participants can lead to increased savings rates when they are encouraged to increase savings rates by at least 2 percentage points and to save at least to the point where they receive the full employer match, if such a match exists.[57] Another service provider told us that it offers an online calculator that managed account participants can use to understand their retirement readiness. The provider also said that participants who use the calculator can see how increased savings can lead to improved retirement outcomes and will often increase their savings rate into their managed account.

Improve Access to Retirement Planning Information

Retirement readiness statements received by participants who are enrolled in a managed account are another reported advantage of the service. Participants generally receive retirement readiness statements that can help them assess whether they are on track to reach their retirement goals, and the statements generally contain information about their retirement investments, savings rate, asset allocations, and projected retirement income. These statements help participants understand the likelihood of reaching their retirement goals given their current investment strategy and whether they should consider increasing their savings rates or changing risk tolerances for their investments. In some cases, these statements may provide participants with their first look in one document at the overall progress they are making toward their retirement goals.[58] As shown in table 3, our review of three providers' statements shows that they use different metrics on participant readiness statements to evaluate participants' retirement prospects. For example, each statement provided participants with information on their retirement goals and risk tolerance, and a projection of their future retirement income to demonstrate the value of the service.

Similar advantages, however, can be achieved through other retirement investment vehicles outside of a managed account and without paying the additional managed account fee. For example, in one recent study, a record keeper that offers managed accounts through its platform showed that there are other ways to diversify using professionally managed allocations, such as target date funds, which can be less costly.[59] Although managed account providers may encourage participants to save more and review their progress towards achieving a secure retirement, participants still have to pay attention to these features of the managed account for it to provide value. Even if 401(k) plan participants are not in managed accounts, we found that in some instances they can still receive advice and education from a provider in the form of retirement readiness statements.

Fees for Managed Accounts Can Be a Disadvantage for Participants

The additional fee a participant generally pays for a managed account was the primary disadvantage mentioned by many industry representatives, plan sponsors, and participant advocates. Because of these additional fees, 401(k) plan participants who do not receive higher investment returns from the managed account services risk losing money over time. Some managed account providers and record keepers have reported that managed account participants earn higher returns than participants who self-direct their 401(k) plan investments, which may help participants offset the additional fee charged. For example, one provider told us that participants enrolled in managed accounts saw about 1.82 percentage points better performance per year, net of fees, compared to participants without managed accounts. Given these higher returns, this provider projects that a 25-year-old enrolled in its managed account could potentially see up to 35 percent more income at retirement than a participant not enrolled in the service, according to this provider's calculations.[60] Another provider reported that the portfolios of participants who were defaulted into managed accounts were projected to receive returns of nearly 1 percentage point more annually, net of fees, after the provider made allocation changes to the participants' portfolios.

However, the higher rates of return projected by managed account providers may not always be achievable. For instance, we found limited data from one record keeper that published returns for managed account participants that were generally less than or equal to the returns of other professionally managed allocations (a single target date fund or balanced fund) as shown in figure 8.[61]

We used these and other returns data published by this record keeper to illustrate the potential effect over 20 years of different rates of return on participant account balances.[62] On the lower end, this record keeper reported that, over a recent 5-year period, 25 percent of its participants earned annualized returns of -0.1 percent or less, not even making up the cost of the additional fee for the service. On the higher end, the record keeper reported that, over a slightly different 5-year period, 25 percent of its participants earned annualized returns of 2.4 percent or higher for the service. These actual returns illustrate the substantial degree to which returns can vary. If such a 2.5 percentage point difference (between these higher and lower reported managed account rates of return of 2.4 percent and -0.1 percent, respectively) were to persist over 20 years, a participant earning the higher managed account rate of return could have nearly 26 percent more in their ending account balance at the end of 20 years than a participant earning the lower rate of return in their managed account.[63] As shown in Figure 9, using these actual rates of return experienced by participants in managed accounts, such a variation in rates of return can substantially affect participant account balances over 20 years.

Table 3. Information in Retirement Readiness Statements Furnished to Participants in Three Managed Accounts that GAO Reviewed

	Provider 1	Provider 2	Provider 3
Participant profile, retirement goals, and/or risk tolerance	✓	✓	✓
Retirement readiness projection and expected monthly or annual retirement income[a]	✓	✓	✓
Current asset allocation	✓	✓	
Opening and closing account balance for the period	✓	✓	
Participant assets and/or liabilities	✓	✓	
Savings rate	✓	✓	✓
Individual fund and aggregate account performance	✓		
Fees	✓		
Action plan to increase savings	✓	✓	✓

Source: GAO analysis of managed account reports reviewed during provider cased studies. | GAO-14-310.

[a] Typically, a projected amount of monthly income in retirement from all sources, including the 401(k) plan, Social Security retirement benefits, and any defined benefit plans.

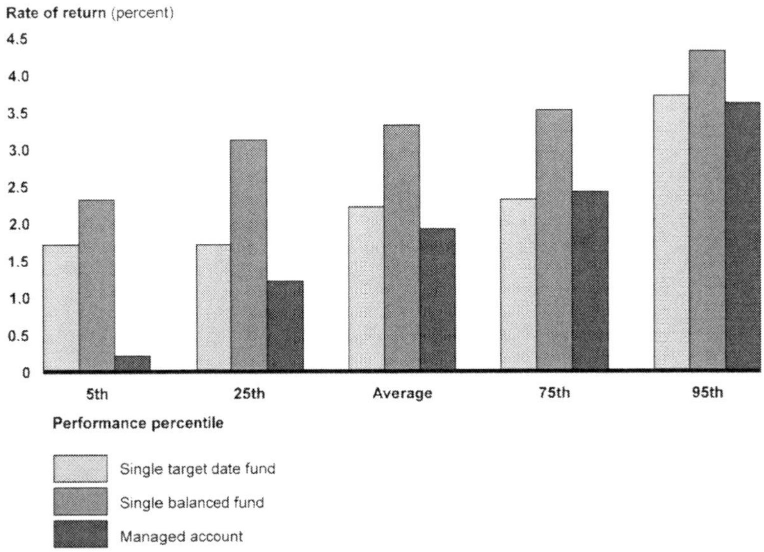

Source: GAO representation of Vanguard returns data. | GAO-14-310.

Note: Information in this record keeper's reports is from a limited dataset that can only describe the portfolio performance for this record keeper's defined contribution plan participants with these types of retirement portfolios over a finite period of time. These data are not representative of the portfolio performance of the universe of defined contribution plan participants or for other periods of time. See Vanguard, *Professionally Managed Allocations and the Dispersion of Participant Portfolios* (Valley Forge, PA: August 2013) and Vanguard, *Target Date Funds and the Dispersion of Participant Portfolios* (Valley Forge, PA: November 2012). These studies examine the effect of professionally managed allocations on participant portfolio construction in defined contribution plans. Professionally managed allocations are participant accounts where 100 percent of the balance is invested by a professional money manager. For these studies, a single target date fund is the most common type of professionally managed allocation, but the category also includes traditional balanced funds and a managed account advisory service. The 5-year returns data include portfolio returns from the recession of 2007-2008. For this reason, the traditional balanced fund had generally higher returns over this period because of their larger fixed income exposure. Return results would likely be different if data from 2007-2008 were not included in the analysis.

Figure 8. Example of Annualized Rates of Return from One Record Keeper for Different Types of Professionally Managed 401(k) Portfolios, 2007-2012, Net of Additional Fees.

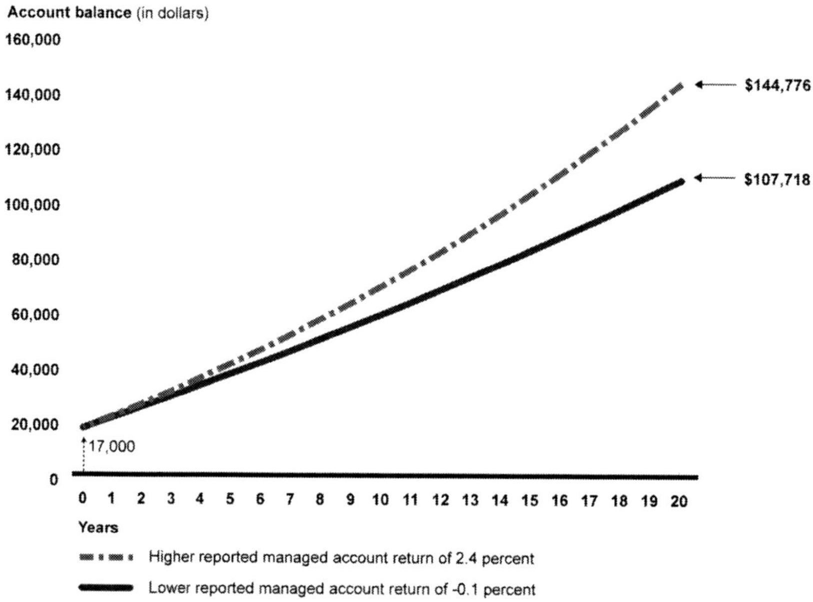

Source: GAO analysis of information from providers and published data on managed account fees and returns. | GAO-14-310.

Note: We conducted this analysis assuming that the participant had a starting account balance of $17,000 (based on the Employee Benefit Research Institute's (EBRI's) estimated median 401(k) account balance at year-end 2011), a starting salary of $40,000 (based on the Bureau of Labor Statistics' seasonally adjusted median weekly earnings for the third quarter of 2013), an average annual salary increase of 1.75 percent (based on the Bureau of Labor Statistics' salary increase estimate for the 12-month period ending September 2013), and a savings rate of 9.7 percent (based on EBRI's estimate of an average employee savings rate of 6.7 percent for 2012 and a 3 percent average employer match). We used Vanguard's published data on 5-year annualized returns for defined contribution plan participants with professionally managed allocations, including managed accounts and participant-constructed portfolios, which we refer to as self-directed 401(k) accounts. The -0.1 percent return represents the 25th percentile in managed account returns performance for the period of 2006-2011. The 2.4 percent return represents the 75th percentile in managed account returns for the period of 2007-2012. The managed account rates of return in this analysis are net of additional fees charged to participants. The 5-year returns data include portfolio returns from the recession of 2007-2008. Return results would likely be different if data from 2007-2008 were not included in the analysis. Information provided by Vanguard is from a limited dataset that can only describe the portfolio performance for Vanguard defined contribution plan participants with these types of retirement portfolios over a finite period of time. These data are not representative of the portfolio performance of the universe of defined contribution plan participants or for other periods of time. See Vanguard, *Professionally Managed Allocations and the Dispersion of Participant Portfolios* (Valley Forge, PA: August 2013) and Vanguard, *Target Date Funds and the Dispersion of Participant Portfolios* (Valley Forge, PA: November 2012).

Figure 9. Example of Growth in a Participant's 401(k) Account Balance over Time Using Different Reported Managed Account Rates of Return, Net of Additional Fees.

Further, this record keeper's published data on managed account rates of return were net of fees—rates of return would be higher if participants did not pay the additional fee for the service. For example, using this record keeper's average fee rate in our analysis,[64] we estimate that a hypothetical managed account participant who earned a higher rate of return of 2.4 percent will pay $8,400 more in additional fees over 20 years than a participant who self-directs investments in their 401(k) account and does not pay the additional fee.[65] To illustrate the potential effect that fees could have on a hypothetical participant's account balance over 20 years, we used a higher fee of 1 percent reported to us by one provider to estimate that a participant would pay $14,000 in additional fees compared to a participant who self-directs investments in their 401(k) account over the same period. However, based on the reported performance data we found, there is no guarantee that participants will earn a higher rate of return with a managed account compared to the returns for other professionally managed allocations or self-directed 401(k) accounts. The limited performance data we reviewed show that in most cases, managed accounts underperformed these other professionally managed allocations and self-directed 401(k) accounts over a 5-year period. However, managed account participants with lower rates of return still pay substantial additional fees for the service. To further illustrate the effect of fees on account balances, a hypothetical participant who earns a lower managed account rate of return of -0.1 percent would pay $6,900 in additional fees using this record keeper's average fee over 20 years compared to a participant who self-directed investments in their 401(k) account, and the additional fees would increase to $11,500 at the 1 percent fee level using the lower rate of return.[66]

The additional managed account fees, which are charged to participants over and above investment management and administrative fees,[67] can vary substantially, and as a result, some participants pay no fees, others pay a flat fee each year, and still others pay a comparatively large percentage of their account balance for generally similar services from managed account providers.[68] In our case studies, we reviewed the additional fees charged to participants for the service. One managed account provider charges a flat rate and fees for the other seven providers ranged from 0.08 to 1 percent of the participant's account balance annually, or $8 to $100 on every $10,000 in a participant's account.[69] Therefore, participants with similar balances but different providers can pay different fees. As shown in table 4, participants with an account balance of $10,000 whose provider charges the highest fee may pay 12.5 times as much as participants whose provider charges the lowest fee ($100 and $8, respectively). However, participants with an account balance of $500,000 may pay up to 250 times as much as other participants but one is subject to a provider who charges the highest fees while the other is at the lowest fee provider ($5,000 and $20, respectively).

Participants with large account balances whose managed account provider caps fees at a certain level benefit more than similar participants whose fees are not capped. Of the providers we reviewed who charge variable fees, one provider caps the fee at a certain amount per year. For example, this provider charges 0.25 percent or $25 for every $10,000 in a participant's account, with a maximum of $250 per year, so participants who use this provider only pay fees on the first $100,000 in their accounts. As a result, the difference in fees paid by participants using this provider, or providers who charge flat rates, widens as participant account balances increase.

Plan characteristics can affect fees participants pay to managed account providers. For example, at one managed account provider included in our review, a participant in a small plan may pay more for a managed account than a similar participant in a large plan. Similarly, a participant in a plan with high enrollment or that uses managed accounts as the default may pay less for a managed account than a participant with the same balance in a plan with low enrollment or that offers managed accounts as an opt-in service. We also found through our case studies that fees can vary based on factors beyond the plan's characteristics, such as the types of providers involved in offering the managed account, the size of participant account balances, and the amount of revenue sharing[70] received by the managed account provider. Fees calculated through revenue sharing can vary in accordance with the investment options the plan sponsor chooses to include in the plan and the amount of revenue the provider actually receives from these options. In these cases, initial fee estimates for the managed account may differ from actual fees they pay. In addition, some plan sponsors also pay fees to offer managed account services, but since these fees may be paid out of plan assets, participants in these plans may pay more than participants in plans that do not pay fees.[71]

Table 4. Example of Variation in 401(k) Plan Managed Account Fees

Provider	Type of fee	Example of annual fee charged on $10,000 account balance	Example of annual fee charged on $500,000 account balance
A	Flat fee	$20	$20
B	Variable fee,[a] capped[b]	$25	$250
C	Variable fee	$10	$500
D	Variable fee, direct arrangement[c]	As low as $8	As low as $400
	Variable fee, subadvised arrangement[d]	As high as $40	As high as $2,000
E	Variable fee, tiered,[e] default[f]	As high as $35	As high as $1,100
	Variable fee, tiered, opt-in[f]	As high as $60	As high as $2,350
F	Variable fee, tiered	Averages $45-$50	Averages $2,250-$2,500
G	Variable fee, default	As low as $45	As low as $2,250
	Variable fee, opt-in	As high as $55	As high as $2,750
H	Variable fee, large plan	As low as $25	As low as $1,250
	Variable fee, small plan	As high as $100	As high as $5,000

Source: GAO analysis of managed account provider case studies. | GAO-14-310.

Note: We estimate that these eight providers chosen for our case studies represented over 95 percent of the managed account industry in defined contribution plans, as measured by assets under management in 2013.

[a] Fees can vary based on a number of factors, such as certain plan characteristics (i.e., the amount of assets in the plan, the percentage of plan participants enrolled in managed accounts) or the level of a participant's account balance.

[b] This provider placed a limit on the fee they charge at a specific dollar amount.

[c] A direct arrangement generally refers to situations where the managed account provider contracts directly with the plan sponsor.

[d] A subadvised arrangement generally describes situations where the managed account provider contracts with another plan services provider. In this arrangement plan sponsors do not contract directly with managed account providers.

[e] Fees may be tiered, meaning that they generally decrease as a participant's account balance increases.

[f] Fees may vary based on whether or not participants are defaulted into managed accounts by the plan sponsor or choose to opt into the managed account service.

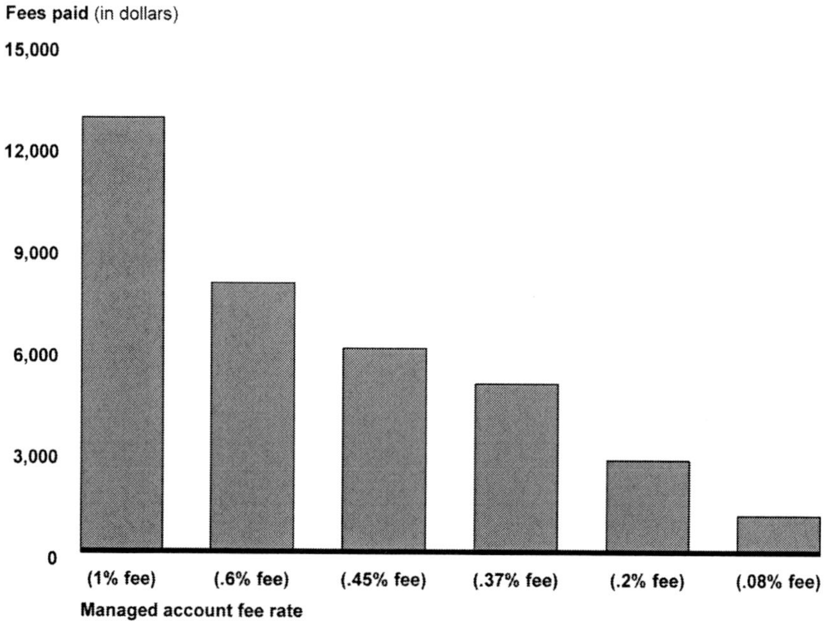

Source: GAO analysis of information from providers and published data on managed account fees and returns. | GAO-14-310.

Note: We conducted this analysis assuming that the participant had a starting account balance of $17,000 (based on the Employee Benefit Research Institute's (EBRI's) estimated median 401(k) account balance at year-end 2011), a starting salary of $40,000 (based on the Bureau of Labor Statistics' seasonally adjusted median weekly earnings for the third quarter of 2013), an average annual salary increase of 1.75 percent (based on the Bureau of Labor Statistics' salary increase estimate for the 12-month period ending September 2013), and a savings rate of 9.7 percent (based on EBRI's estimate of an average employee savings rate of 6.7 percent for 2012 and a 3 percent average employer match). This participant invested over 20 years using a managed account service with an annual rate of return of 1.9 percent, which represents an average of the average rates of return earned by participants with self-directed 401(k) accounts published by Vanguard in its 401(k) performance reports for the periods of 2006-2011 and 2007-2012. We used Vanguard's published data on 5-year annualized returns for defined contribution plan participants with professionally managed allocations, including managed accounts, and participant-constructed portfolios, which we refer to as self-directed 401(k) accounts. The 5-year returns data include portfolio returns from the recession of 2007-2008. Return results would likely be different if data from 2007-2008 were not included in the analysis. Information provided by Vanguard is from a limited dataset that can only describe the portfolio performance for Vanguard defined contribution plan participants with these types of retirement portfolios over a finite period of time. These data are not representative of the portfolio performance of the universe of defined contribution plan participants or for other periods of time. See Vanguard, *Professionally Managed Allocations and the Dispersion of Participant Portfolios* (Valley Forge, PA: August 2013) and Vanguard, *Target Date Funds and the Dispersion of Participant Portfolios* (Valley Forge, PA: November 2012).

Figure 10. Variation in Additional Participant Fees Paid for a Managed Account Over a 20-Year Period Given Different Fee Rates.

As shown above, paying higher additional fees to a provider for a managed account service offers no guarantee of higher rates of return compared to other providers or compared to the reported rates of return earned by participants who invest in other professionally managed allocations or who self-direct investments in their 401(k) accounts. Because the additional fee is charged to participants on a recurring basis, such as every quarter or year, the costs incurred over time by participants who use managed accounts can accumulate. We used fee data reported by managed account providers to illustrate the effect that different fees could have on a participant's managed account balance over time. As shown in figure 10, a hypothetical participant in our illustration who is charged an additional annual fee of 1 percent of their account balance for their managed account may pay nearly $13,000 more over 20 years than they would have paid in any other investment without the managed account fee. This compares to about $1,100 in additional fees paid over 20 years by a participant who is charged an annual fee of 0.08 percent for a managed account, the lowest variable non-capped fee we found.[72]

Lack of a Requirement for Performance and Benchmarking Information Inhibits Participant Evaluation of Managed Accounts

The limited availability of returns-based performance data and lack of standard metrics can also offset the reported advantages of managed accounts. In its final rule on participant-level disclosures, DOL requires that sponsors disclose performance data to help participants make informed decisions about the management of their individual accounts and the investment of their retirement savings, and that sponsors provide appropriate benchmarks to help participants assess the various investment options available under their plan.[73] By requiring sponsors to provide participants with performance data and benchmarking information for 401(k) investments, DOL intends to reduce the time required for participants to collect and organize fee and performance information and increase participants' efficiency in choosing investment options that will provide the highest value.

Table 5. Examples of Plan and Investment-Related Information Plan Sponsors Are Required to Disclose to Participants with 401(k) Investments

Type of information	Requirement
Identifying information	• The name of each designated investment alternative[a] • The type or category of the investment (e.g., money market fund, balanced fund (stocks and bonds), large cap stock fund, employer stock fund, employer securities).
Performance data[b]	• For designated investment alternatives with respect to which the return is not fixed, the average annual total return of the investment for 1-, 5-, and 10-calendar year periods (or for the life of the alternative, if shorter) ending on the date of the most recently completed calendar year. • A statement indicating that an investment's past performance is not necessarily an indication of how the investment will perform in the future.
Benchmarks[b]	• Standard: For designated investment alternatives with respect to which the return is not fixed, the name and returns of an appropriate broad based securities market index over the 1-, 5-, and 10-calendar year periods (or for the life of the alternative, if shorter), which is not administered by an affiliate of the investment issuer, its investment adviser, or a principal underwriter, unless the index is widely recognized and used. • Custom: In the case of designated investment alternatives that have a mix of equity and fixed income exposure (e.g., balanced funds or target date funds), a plan administrator may blend the returns of more than one appropriate broad-based index and present the blended returns along with the returns of the required benchmark, provided that the blended returns reflect the proportion of actual equity and fixed-income holdings of the designated investment alternative. For example, where a balanced fund's equity-to-bond ratio is 60:40, the returns of an appropriate bond index and an appropriate equity index may be blended in the same ratio and presented along with the benchmark returns.

Source: GAO analysis of DOL regulations at 29 C.F.R. § 2550.404a-5(d)(1)(i),(ii), and (iii). | GAO-14-310.

[a] DOL defines a designated investment alternative as "any investment alternative designated by the plan into which participants and beneficiaries may direct the

investment of assets held in, or contributed to, their individual accounts." 29 C.F.R. § 2550.404a-5(h)(4).

[b] Plan sponsors are required to furnish this information to participants in a chart or similar format that is designed to facilitate comparison of such information for each designated investment alternative offered under the plan. 29 C.F.R. § 2550.404a-5(d)(2)(i). The final rule includes a Model Comparative Chart plan sponsors may elect to use to satisfy this requirement. See 75 Fed. Reg. 64,942.

Since the applicability date of the participant-level disclosure regulation, for most plans in 2012, DOL has required plan sponsors to provide participants who invest in a "designated investment alternative" in their 401(k) account with an annual disclosure describing the fees, expenses, and performance of each of the investment funds available to them in the plan.[74] DOL defines a designated investment alternative as "any investment alternative designated by the plan into which participants and beneficiaries may direct the investment of assets held in, or contributed to, their individual accounts."[75] For designated investment alternatives, plan sponsors are required to disclose to participants specific information identifying the funds available to them in the plan, results-based performance information over varying time periods, and performance benchmarks in a way that invites comparison with established benchmarks and market indexes, as shown in table 5.

Despite DOL's requirements for designated investment alternatives, with respect to managed accounts offered either as an opt-in or default service, plan sponsors are generally only required to disclose to 401(k) participants the identity of the managed account provider or investment manager and any fees and expenses associated with its management. Neither plan sponsors nor managed account providers are required to isolate within the participant-level disclosure investment-related information on the individual funds that comprise the participant's managed account or present aggregate performance of the account for a given period. DOL generally does not consider most managed accounts to be "designated investment alternatives." Instead, according to DOL, managed account providers are generally considered to be "designated investment managers" as they provide a service to participants rather than an investment option, such as a mutual fund.[76] As a result, the investment–related information required in DOL's participant-level disclosure regulation does not apply to investment services, such as many managed accounts.

Because DOL does not require plan sponsors to provide participants information on the performance of their managed accounts or to compare performance against a set of standard benchmarks, it is potentially difficult for participants to evaluate whether the additional fees for managed accounts are worth paying, considering the effect of fees on returns and retirement account balances. As a result, participants may be unable to effectively assess the overall value of the service and to compare performance against a set of standard benchmarks. Not all of the retirement readiness statements we reviewed included returns-based performance data or information on the amount of additional fees the participant had paid for the service.[77] Some managed account providers did include projections of a participant's future retirement income on these statements. Even though the projections may be based on sound methodologies, if standard returns-based performance data are absent from these statements, participants will have to rely primarily on these projections to gauge the overall value of the service. Without performance and benchmarking information presented in a format designed to help participants compare and evaluate their managed account, participants cannot make informed decisions about the managed account service.

Likewise, with respect to QDIAs, DOL only requires plan sponsors to disclose to participants a description of each investment's objectives, risk and return characteristics (if applicable), fees and expenses paid to providers, and the right of the participant to elect not to have such contributions made on their behalf, among other things.[78] In 2010, DOL proposed amendments to its QDIA disclosure requirements that would, with respect to target date funds or similar investments, require sponsors to provide participants historical returns-based performance data (e.g., 1-, 5-, and 10-year returns).[79] According to DOL officials, the proposed QDIA rule change may apply to managed accounts offered as a QDIA to participants. However, the proposed requirements as written may be difficult for plan sponsors to implement because they are not tailored specifically for managed accounts.[80] One participant advocacy group noted that, without similar information, participants may not be able to effectively assess managed account performance over time and compare that performance to other professionally managed investment options available under the plan or across different managed account providers.[81]

As mentioned above, DOL affirms in the participant-level disclosure regulation that performance data are required to help participants in 401(k) plans to make informed decisions about managing investments in their retirement accounts, and that appropriate benchmarks are helpful tools participants can use to assess the various investment options available under their plan.[82] The benefits outlined in the participant-level disclosure regulation would also apply to the proposed changes to the QDIA regulation. Specifically, DOL expects that the enhanced disclosures required by the proposed regulation would benefit participants by providing them with critical information they need to evaluate the quality of investments offered as QDIAs, leading to improved investment results and retirement planning decisions by participants. DOL believes that the disclosures under the proposed regulation, combined with performance reporting requirement in the participant-level disclosure regulation, would allow participants to determine whether efficiencies gained through these investments are worth the price differential participants generally would pay for such funds. However, absent DOL requirements that plan sponsors use standard metrics to report on the performance of managed accounts for participants who are defaulted into the service as a QDIA, it would be potentially difficult for these participants to evaluate the effect that additional fees could have on the performance of their managed accounts, including how the additional fees could affect returns and retirement account balances, possibly eroding the value of the service over time for those participants.

Improved performance reporting could help participants understand the risks associated with the additional fees and possible effects on their retirement account balances if the managed accounts underperform, which is critical information that participants could use to take action to mitigate those risks. Discussions with managed account providers suggest that returns-based performance reports and custom benchmarking can be provided to managed account participants.[83] For example, as shown in figure 11, one managed account provider we spoke to already furnishes participants access to online reports that include returns-based performance data and custom benchmarks, which can allow them to compare performance for a given period with an established equity index and bond index. Some providers told us that it would be difficult to provide participants in managed accounts with performance information and benchmarks because their retirement portfolios contain highly personalized asset allocations. While it may be more challenging for providers to furnish performance information on personalized managed accounts compared to model portfolios, we identified one participant statement that included performance information from a provider who personalizes asset allocations for their participants' retirement portfolios.

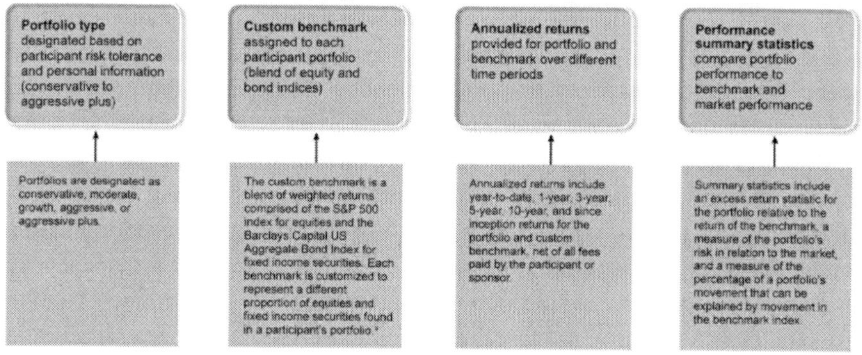

Source: R.T. Jones Capital Equities Management, Inc. | GAO14-310.

[a] For example, if a portfolio designated as "growth" is made of approximately 80 percent equity assets and 20 percent fixed income assets, then the corresponding blended custom benchmark could be comprised of a weighted average of 80 percent S&P 500 index performance and 20 percent Barclays Capital U.S. Aggregate Bond index performance. Custom benchmarks for other portfolio types correspond similarly.

Figure 11. Example of Custom Benchmarks and Summary Statistics Used to Report Managed Account Performance to Participants.

The provider told us that the blended custom benchmark described in figure 11 allows participants to more accurately evaluate and compare the aggregate performance of the different individual funds held in their managed account because the benchmark is linked to the participant's risk tolerance. The online report also describes any positive or negative excess returns for the portfolio relative to the return of the custom benchmark, net of fees. The provider said that the excess return statistic is representative of the value that the provider or portfolio manager has added or subtracted from the participant's portfolio return for a given period.[84] Another managed account provider furnishes retirement readiness statements that include returns-based information for each of the funds in participants' accounts. However, the statement did not include standard or custom benchmarks that would allow participants to compare the performance of their managed account with other market indexes.

ABSENT GUIDANCE, SPONSORS FACE CHALLENGES IN SELECTING AND OVERSEEING MANAGED ACCOUNT PROVIDERS

DOL Has Not Addressed Sponsor Access to Managed Account Provider Options

Some sponsors report that their choice of a managed account provider may be limited to those options—sometimes only one—offered by the plan's record keeper.[85] Although DOL's general guidance on fiduciary responsibilities encourages sponsors to consider several potential providers before hiring one,[86] six of the 10 sponsors we interviewed said that they selected a managed account provider offered by their record keeper without considering other options and two other sponsors said that their record keeper's capabilities partially restricted their choice of a provider. Some record keepers voluntarily offered sponsors more managed account provider options when sponsors asked for them.[87] In the absence of DOL requiring sponsors to request multiple provider options, sponsors said they were reluctant to pursue options not offered by their record keeper for a variety of reasons. These reasons included: (1) concern that their record keeper's systems might be unable to support additional options; (2) familiarity with the current provider offered by their record keeper;[88] and (3) belief that there was no need to consider other options—one sponsor said that its record keeper has consistently provided excellent service and support for a reasonable fee and, as a result, the sponsor felt comfortable accepting the record keeper's recommendation of the provider offered on its recordkeeping system.

Without the ability to choose among multiple providers, sponsors have limited choices, which can result in selecting a provider who charges participants higher additional fees than other providers who use comparable strategies to manage participant investments, which are ultimately deducted from participant account balances. In addition, limited choices can result in sponsors selecting a provider whose strategy does not align with their preferred approach for investing participant contributions. For example, a sponsor who endorses a conservative investment philosophy for their plan could select a provider who uses a more aggressive method for managing participant investments.

Several managed account providers and record keepers said that a limited number of providers are offered because, among other things, it is costly to integrate 401(k) recordkeeping systems with managed account provider systems. In addition, record keepers may offer a limited number of providers to avoid losing revenue and because they evaluate a provider before deciding to offer its managed account service. Such steps include reviewing the provider's investment strategy and assessing how the provider interacts with participants. One managed account provider estimated that sponsors might have to spend $400,000 and wait more than a year before offering the provider's managed account to plan participants if it is not already available on their record keeper's system. Additionally, record keepers may lose target date fund revenue or forgo higher revenue opportunities by offering certain managed account providers and may believe that offering multiple options is unnecessary once they have identified a provider that is effective.

Although sponsors may have access to a limited number of managed account providers on their record keepers' systems, some providers have developed approaches that make it easier for record keepers to offer more than one managed account option to sponsors. For instance, one provider we interviewed, which acts as an intermediary and fiduciary, contracts with several other providers and makes all of these providers available to its record keepers, thus allowing the record keepers' sponsors to choose among several managed account providers without incurring additional costs to integrate the record keeper with any of the providers.[89] Another managed account provider has developed a process to transfer information to record keepers that does not require integration with the recordkeeping system, thus making it less difficult for any record keeper to work with them.

Sponsors Lack Sufficient Guidance from DOL to Inform Their Selection and Oversight of Managed Account Providers

Available evidence we reviewed suggests that sponsors lack sufficient guidance on how to select and oversee managed account providers. Several of the sponsors we interviewed said that they were unaware of any set list of standards for overseeing managed accounts, so they do not follow any standards, and even managed account providers felt that sponsors have insufficient knowledge and information to effectively select a provider. Because sponsors may not have sufficient knowledge and information, record keepers could play a larger role in the selection process. In addition, providers indicated that it is difficult for sponsors to compare providers and attributed this difficulty to the absence of any widely accepted benchmarks or other comparison tools for sponsors. Some industry representatives indicated that additional guidance could help sponsors better select and oversee managed account providers and highlighted specific areas in which guidance would be beneficial, such as:

- determining whether a managed account fee is reasonable;
- understanding managed accounts and how they function; and
- clarifying factors sponsors should consider when selecting a managed account provider.

Although DOL is responsible for assisting and educating sponsors by providing them with guidance, it has not issued guidance specific to managed accounts, as it has done for target date funds,[90] even though it has issued general guidance on fiduciary responsibilities, including regulations under ERISA 404(a) and 404(c), which explicitly state DOL's long-standing position that nothing in either regulation serves to relieve a fiduciary from its duty to prudently select and monitor any service provider to the plan. DOL guidance on target date funds outlines the factors sponsors should consider when selecting and monitoring target date funds, such as performance and fees, among other things. The absence of similar guidance specific to managed accounts has led to inconsistency in sponsors' procedures for selecting and overseeing providers and may inhibit their ability to select a provider who offers an effective service for a reasonable fee. Specifically, without assistance regarding what they should focus on, sponsors may not be considering factors that DOL considers relevant for making fiduciary decisions, such as performance information. For example, sponsors considered a range of factors when selecting a managed account provider, including record keeper views on the quality of the provider, the provider's willingness to serve as a fiduciary, and the managed account provider's investment strategy. In addition, as shown in table 6, while nearly all of the sponsors said that they considered fees when selecting a managed account provider, only 1 of the 10 sponsors we interviewed said that they considered performance information when selecting a managed account provider. In addition, only half of the sponsors we interviewed reported that they take steps to formally benchmark fees by, for example, comparing their participants' fees to the amount of fees that participants in similarly-sized organizations pay.

The extent to which sponsors oversee managed account providers also varies. Nearly all of the 10 sponsors we interviewed said that they review reports from their managed account provider or record keeper as part of their oversight process, and the managed account providers we interviewed highlighted the role that these reports play in the oversight process.[91] Several of these providers noted that the reports they provide help sponsors fulfill their fiduciary responsibility for oversight. Most sponsors said that they also take other steps to oversee managed account providers, such as regularly meeting with them. However, only one sponsor said that, as part of its oversight activities, it independently evaluates benchmarks, such as stock market performance indexes. In addition, even though participants generally pay an additional fee for managed account services, not all of the sponsors we interviewed said that they monitor fees.

Inconsistent Performance Information Allowed by DOL Hinders Sponsor Evaluation of Managed Accounts

Some industry representatives indicated that consistent performance information could help sponsors more effectively compare prospective managed account providers and ultimately improve selection and oversight. Similar to the challenges participants face in evaluating managed accounts because of a lack of performance information, industry representatives said that sponsors need information as well, including:

- useful, comparative performance information and a standard set of metrics to select suitable providers;
- access to standard performance benchmarks to monitor them; and
- access to comparable managed account performance information to evaluate performance.

Some providers highlighted challenges with providing performance information on managed accounts and, as a result, furnish sponsors with other types of information to demonstrate their value to participants. For example, providers may not furnish returns-based performance information to demonstrate how their offerings have affected participants because the personalized nature of managed accounts makes it difficult to measure performance. In lieu of providing returns-based performance information, providers furnish sponsors with changes in portfolio risk levels and diversification, changes in participant savings rates, and retirement readiness. One managed account provider said that it does not believe there is a way to measure the performance of managed accounts, noting that it develops 20 to 50 investment portfolios for any given plan based on the investment options available in the plan.

Table 6. Comparison of Factors Sponsors Said They Considered When Selecting a Managed Account Provider

Factors considered	Sponsors									
	1	2	3	4	5	6	7	8	9	10
1. Fees	X	X	X	X	X	X	X	X	X	[a]
2. Provider's investment strategy	X	X	X	X			X			
3. Provider's ability to work with the plan's record keeper	X		X		X				X	
4. Provider's ability to meet the needs of the sponsor's workforce	X		X	X						X
5. Provider's independence		X	X		X		X			
6. Provider's willingness to serve as a fiduciary	X			X	X					
7. Provider reporting	X	X								
8. Record keeper views on the provider						X		X		
9. Overall quality of provider's services relative to others								X	X	
10. Provider's size/share of the industry	X	X								
11. Provider's ability to accommodate the plan's investment options	X									
12. Ability of participants to opt out of the managed account service						X				
13. Familiarity with provider										X
14. Returns-based performance information										X

Source: GAO analysis of information obtained from interviews with sponsors. | GAO-14-310.

Note: To select sponsors for semi-structured interviews, we conducted a non-generalizable survey because a comprehensive list of plan sponsors that offer managed accounts did not exist at the time of our review. We selected sponsors with a variety of characteristics such as plan size (amount of assets in the plan and number of participants in the plan), managed account provider used, and method for enrolling participants into the managed account service (default or opt-in). See appendix I for additional information on our approach for selecting sponsors.

[a] This sponsor said that its managed account provider does not charge participants an additional fee for managed account services. Thus, fees were not a concern for this sponsor.

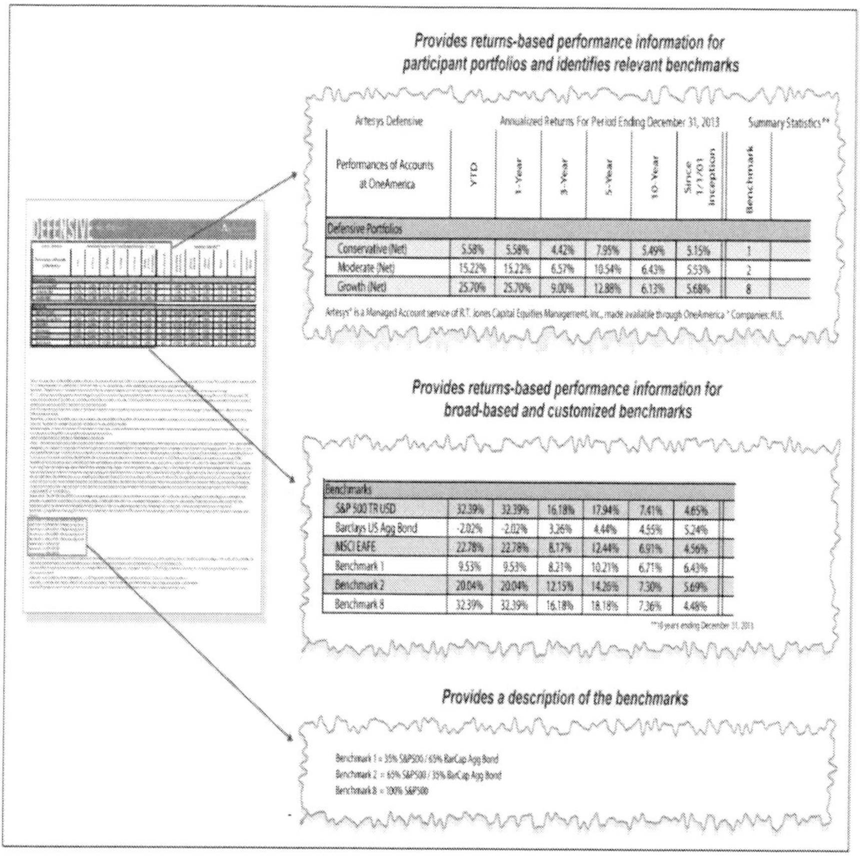

Performances of Accounts at OneAmerica	YTD	1-Year	3-Year	5-Year	10-Year	Since 1/1/01 inception	Benchmark
Defensive Portfolios							
Conservative (Net)	5.58%	5.58%	4.42%	7.95%	5.49%	5.15%	1
Moderate (Net)	15.22%	15.22%	6.57%	10.54%	6.43%	5.53%	2
Growth (Net)	25.70%	25.70%	9.00%	12.88%	6.13%	5.68%	8

Benchmarks						
S&P 500 TR USD	32.39%	32.39%	16.18%	17.94%	7.41%	4.65%
Barclays US Agg Bond	-2.02%	-2.02%	3.26%	4.44%	4.55%	5.24%
MSCI EAFE	22.78%	22.78%	8.17%	12.44%	6.91%	4.56%
Benchmark 1	9.53%	9.53%	8.21%	10.21%	6.71%	6.43%
Benchmark 2	20.04%	20.04%	12.15%	14.26%	7.30%	5.69%
Benchmark 8	32.39%	32.39%	16.18%	18.18%	7.36%	4.48%

Source: R.T. Jones Capital Equities Management, Inc. | GAO-14-310.

Figure 12. Example of Returns-Based Performance Information Provided to Sponsors by One Provider.

Nonetheless, a few providers voluntarily furnish sponsors with returns-based performance information.[92] One provider that used broad-based market indexes and customized benchmarks noted that it would be difficult for a sponsor to select a managed account provider without being able to judge how the provider has performed in the past. In addition, this provider, unlike some other providers, noted that the personalized nature of some managed accounts does not preclude managed account providers from being able to generate returns-based performance information. For example, even though plans may differ, providers can collect information from record keepers for each of the plans that offer managed accounts and create aggregate returns data, which could then be disclosed to sponsors along with an explanation of how the data were generated. As shown in figure 12, the report that this provider distributes to sponsors contains an array of performance information for participant portfolios, including rates of return earned by the portfolios for multiple time periods and benchmarks. In addition, the report provides a description of the benchmarks—broad-based market indexes as well as customized benchmarks.

DOL regulations require that service providers furnish sponsors with performance and benchmarking information for the investment options available in the plan.[93] DOL maintains that sponsors need this information in order to make better decisions when selecting and monitoring providers for their plans. However, DOL regulations generally do not require managed account providers to furnish sponsors with performance and benchmarking information for managed accounts because, as previously noted, managed accounts are not considered to be designated investment alternatives. Without this information, sponsors cannot effectively compare different providers when making a selection or adequately determine whether their managed account offerings are having a positive effect on participant retirement savings, as they can currently determine with the designated investment alternatives available in the plan.

CONCLUSION

Managed accounts can be useful services and may offer some advantages for 401(k) participants. They build diversified portfolios for participants, help them make investment decisions, select appropriate asset allocations, and estimate the amount they need to contribute to achieve a secure retirement. Given these potential advantages, it is no surprise that the number of managed account providers has grown and that plan sponsors, seeking to provide the best options for plan participants, have increasingly offered managed accounts. The extent to which managed accounts benefit participants may depend on the participant's level of engagement and ability to increase their savings. Despite the potential advantages, better protections are needed to ensure that participants realize their retirement goals. These protections are especially important as additional fees for this service can slow or erode participants' accumulated retirement savings over time.

Helping plan sponsors understand and make appropriate decisions about managed accounts can better ensure that participants are able to reap the full advantages of managed accounts. Since plan sponsors select a managed account provider, participants who use these services are subject to that managed account provider's structure and strategies for allocating participant assets, which can potentially affect participants' ability to save for retirement, especially if they pay high fees. Some participants cannot be assured that they are receiving impartial managed account services or are able to rely on accountable investment professionals taking on appropriate fiduciary responsibilities. Clarifying fiduciary roles for providers who offer managed accounts to participants on an opt-in basis or for providers who offer additional services to participants in or near retirement could help ensure that sponsors have a clear understanding of provider responsibilities so they can offer the best services to their participants.

DOL can also help sponsors gain clarity and confidence in selecting and monitoring managed account providers. This is particularly salient since managed accounts can be complicated service arrangements and there are considerable structural differences among the managed account options offered by providers. By requiring sponsors to request multiple provider options from their record keeper, DOL can help ensure that sponsors thoroughly evaluate managed account providers before they are offered to participants. In addition, providing sponsors with guidance that clarifies standards and suggests actions for prudently selecting and overseeing managed account providers, such as documenting their processes and understanding the strategies used in the managed account, positions sponsors to better navigate their fiduciary responsibilities. Additional guidance also positions sponsors to consider additional factors when choosing to default participants into managed accounts. Supplementing this guidance by requiring providers to furnish consistent performance information to sponsors so that they can more effectively compare providers can assist sponsors in their efforts to provide a beneficial service that could help preserve and potentially enhance participants' retirement security.

Finally, DOL can also help participants evaluate whether their managed account service is beneficial. Without standardized performance and benchmarking information, participants may not be able to effectively assess the performance of their managed account and determine whether the additional fee for the service is worth paying. For participants who opt into managed accounts, this information could help them more effectively assess the performance of their managed account and compare that performance to other professionally managed alternatives that may be less expensive, such as target date funds. Alternatively, for participants who are defaulted into managed accounts, this information could be valuable when they start to pay more attention to their retirement savings.

RECOMMENDATIONS FOR EXECUTIVE ACTION

To better protect plan sponsors and participants who use managed account services, we recommend that the Secretary of Labor direct the Assistant Secretary for the Employee Benefits Security Administration (EBSA) to:

a) Review provider practices related to additional managed account services offered to participants in or near retirement, with the aim of determining whether conflicts of interest exist and, if it determines it is necessary, taking the appropriate action to remedy the issue.
b) Consider the fiduciary status of managed account providers when they offer services on an opt-in basis and, if necessary, make regulatory changes or provide guidance to address any issues.

To help sponsors who offer managed account services or who are considering doing so better protect their 401(k) plan participants, we recommend that the Secretary of Labor direct the Assistant Secretary for EBSA to:

c) Provide guidance to plan sponsors for selecting and overseeing managed account providers that addresses: (1) the importance of considering multiple providers when choosing a managed account provider, (2) factors to consider when offering managed accounts as a QDIA or on an opt-in basis, and (3) approaches for evaluating the services of managed account providers.
d) Require plan sponsors to request from record keepers more than one managed account provider option, and notify the Department of Labor if record keepers fail to do so.

To help sponsors and participants more effectively assess the performance of managed accounts, we recommend that the Secretary of Labor direct the Assistant Secretary for EBSA to:

e) Amend participant disclosure regulations to require that sponsors furnish standardized performance and benchmarking information to participants. To accomplish this, EBSA could promulgate regulations that would require sponsors who offer managed account services to provide their participants with standardized performance and benchmarking information on managed accounts. For example, sponsors could periodically furnish each managed account participant with the aggregate performance of participants' managed account portfolios and returns for broad- based securities market indexes and applicable customized benchmarks, based on those benchmarks provided for the plan's designated investment alternatives.

f) Amend service provider disclosure regulations to require that providers furnish standardized performance and benchmarking information to sponsors. To accomplish this, EBSA could promulgate regulations that would require service providers to disclose to sponsors standardized performance and benchmarking information on managed accounts. For example, providers could, prior to selection and periodically thereafter, as applicable, furnish sponsors with aggregated returns for generalized conservative, moderate, and aggressive portfolios, actual managed account portfolio returns for each of the sponsor's participants, and returns for broad-based securities market indexes and applicable customized benchmarks, based on those benchmarks provided for the plan's designated investment alternatives.

AGENCY COMMENTS AND OUR EVALUATION

We provided a draft of this report to the Department of Labor, the Department of the Treasury, the Securities and Exchange Commission, and the Consumer Financial Protection Bureau for review and comment. The Department of the Treasury and the Consumer Financial Protection Bureau did not have any comments. DOL and SEC provided technical comments, which we have incorporated where appropriate. DOL also provided written comments. As stated in its letter, DOL agreed with our recommendations and will consider each of them as it moves forward with a number of projects.

In response to our recommendation that DOL review provider practices related to additional managed account services offered to participants in or near retirement to determine whether conflicts of interest exist, DOL agreed to include these practices in its current review of investment advice conflicts of interest, noting that such conflicts continue to be a concern. Regarding our second recommendation, to consider the fiduciary status of managed account providers when they offer services on an opt-in basis, DOL agreed to review existing guidance and consider whether additional guidance is needed in light of the various business models we described. By considering managed account service provider practices and fiduciary roles in its current efforts and taking any necessary action to address potential issues, we believe DOL will help ensure that sponsors and participants receive unconflicted managed account services from qualified managers.

DOL also agreed to consider our other recommendations in connection with its current regulatory project on standards for brokerage windows in participant-directed individual account plans. We believe that this project may be a good starting point for requesting additional information and considering adjustments to those managed account services participants obtain from advisers through brokerage windows. As we noted in our report, we did not include these types of managed accounts in our review because the plan sponsor is not usually involved in the selection and monitoring of these advisers. Since participants can obtain managed account services without using a brokerage window, we encourage DOL to also consider our third and fourth recommendations outside of the context of brokerage windows. Providing guidance to sponsors for selecting and overseeing managed account providers, as suggested by our third recommendation, may help sponsors understand their fiduciary responsibilities with respect to managed accounts. Similarly, requiring plan sponsors to ask for more than one choice of managed account provider, as suggested by our fourth recommendation, could encourage record keepers to offer additional choices. By taking the steps outlined in these recommendations, DOL can help ensure that participants are being offered effective managed account services for reasonable fees.

With respect to our recommendation requiring plan sponsors to ask for more than one choice of managed account provider, DOL noted that it needs to review the extent of its legal authority to effectively require plans to have more than one managed account service provider. We continue to believe that the action we suggest in our recommendation—that DOL simply require plan sponsors to *ask* for more than one *choice* of a provider, which is slightly different than how DOL has characterized it— may be an effective method of broadening plan sponsors' choices of managed account providers. However, we agree that DOL should examine the scope of its existing authority in considering how it might implement this recommendation.

Finally, DOL agreed to consider our recommendations on the disclosure of performance and benchmarking information on managed accounts to participants and sponsors in connection with its open proposed rulemaking project involving the qualified default investment alternative and participant-level disclosure regulations. We believe that DOL's consideration of these recommendations in connection with this rulemaking project will be helpful for participants and sponsors, and encourage DOL to include managed accounts in this rulemaking. Although managed accounts are different than target date funds in multiple ways, as presented in our report, we believe that managed account providers can and should provide some level of performance and benchmarking information to sponsors—and sponsors to participants—to describe how managed accounts perform over time and the risks associated with the service. In addition, to the extent that managed accounts offered on an opt-in basis are not covered by DOL's project, we encourage DOL to consider adopting similar changes to the participant- level disclosures for those managed accounts that are not governed by QDIA regulations.

Sincerely yours,

Charles A. Jeszeck
Director
Education, Workforce, and Income Security

APPENDIX I: OBJECTIVES, SCOPE, AND METHODOLOGY

Our objectives for this study were to determine (1) how service providers structure managed accounts, (2) the advantages and disadvantages of managed accounts for 401(k) participants, and (3) the challenges, if any, that plan sponsors face in selecting and overseeing managed account providers.

To answer our research objectives we undertook several different approaches. We reviewed relevant research and federal laws, regulations, and guidance on managed accounts in 401(k) plans. We reviewed available documentation on the structure of managed accounts in 401(k) plans and the role of service providers, including Securities and Exchange Commission (SEC) filings of the Form ADV by 30 record keepers, managed account providers, and other related service providers.[94] We interviewed industry representatives and service providers involved with managed accounts—including record keepers, academics, industry research firms, and participant advocacy groups—and government officials from the Department of Labor's

Employee Benefits Security Administration (EBSA), SEC, the Department of the Treasury, and the Consumer Financial Protection Bureau.

Case Studies of Managed Account Providers

To examine key issues related to how managed accounts in 401(k) plans are structured, we conducted in-depth case studies of eight selected managed account providers.[95] Since we were unable to identify a comprehensive list of managed account providers that provide services to 401(k) plans, to select providers for case studies we first developed a list of 14 managed account providers based on discussions with two industry research firms and our own analysis of information from record keeper websites and other publicly available documentation. To assess the reliability of these data, we interviewed the two industry research firms and compared their information with the results of our analysis for corroboration and reasonableness. We determined that the data we used were sufficiently reliable for selecting managed account providers for case studies. From the list of 14 providers, we selected 10 providers based on their size, location, and legal and fee structures, from which we used eight as the basis for our case studies. According to our estimates, the eight managed account providers we included in the case studies represented over 95 percent of the managed account industry in defined contribution plans, as measured by assets under management in 2013.

In conducting case studies of managed account providers, we interviewed representatives of the managed account provider and chose five providers for site visits based on their locations and size. We also reviewed publicly available documentation describing the nature of the managed account and sample reports furnished by providers, confirmed the type of information these providers consider when managing a participant's account, and analyzed fee data furnished by managed account providers. To assess the reliability of the fee data furnished by managed account providers, we corroborated and assessed the completeness of reported fee data based on information in provider SEC filings and any other relevant documentary evidence, when possible. We determined that the data were sufficiently reliable for depicting the range and types of fees charged to sponsors and participants by providers. In addition, to further understand the different strategies and structures of managed accounts, we developed and submitted five hypothetical participant scenarios in one hypothetical plan to the eight service providers and asked them to provide example asset allocations, and advice if practical, for those participants. Seven of the eight managed account providers completed and returned asset allocations to us. See appendix II for additional detail on the development of hypothetical scenarios and results from this work.

Illustrations of Fee and Return Data Over Time

To illustrate potential performance outcomes for participants in managed accounts, we used available data on actual managed account rates of return and fees to show how managed accounts could affect 401(k) account balances over 20 years. We developed two scenarios, isolating the effects of variability in the following factors:

1. Managed account rates of return – We used annual average managed account rates of return ranging from -0.1 percent to 2.4 percent, based on published performance data.[96] We compared the change in account balances for those managed account rates of return with the change in account balances for a 1.4 percent rate of return experienced by participants who directed their own 401(k) investments.
2. Managed account fees – We used different fee levels obtained from published reports and provider interviews ranging from a low additional annual fee of 0.08 percent to a 1 percent annual fee.[97] We compared fee totals and ending account balances for varying fee levels with those of participants who did not pay the additional fee because they directed their own 401(k) investments.

For each scenario, we held all other factors constant by assuming that the participant's starting account balance was $17,000 and starting salary was $40,000, the salary increased at a rate of 1.75 percent per year, and the participant saved 9.7 percent[98] of their salary each year.[99] To the extent possible, we developed scenarios using information provided to us during interviews with industry representatives or found in published reports on managed accounts or on other economic factors. To assess the reliability of these data, we considered the reliability and familiarity of the source of the data or information and, when necessary, interviewed representatives of those sources about their methods, internal controls, and results. Based on these interviews and our review of published data, we determined that the data we used were sufficiently reliable for use in these illustrations.

Because this work presents simplified illustrations of potential effects on participants over time, we used nominal dollar amounts over 20 years and did not take into account inflation or changes in interest rates. Similarly, to minimize effects of percentage growth/loss sequencing on account balances, we applied the same rates of return to each of the 20 years for each scenario. The rates of returns we used in both scenarios already incorporated different asset allocations for participants with a managed account or a self-directed 401(k) account. This work does not attempt to specify or adjust these specific asset allocations.

Semi-Structured Interviews with Plan Sponsors

To identify the advantages and disadvantages of managed accounts for 401(k) plan participants and any challenges sponsors face in selecting and overseeing managed account providers, we conducted semi-structured interviews with 12 plan sponsors. Our process for interviewing plan sponsors involved multiple steps, as outlined below.

Sponsor Selection

Since a comprehensive list of sponsors that managed accounts did not exist at the time of our review, to select sponsors for semi-structured interviews, we conducted a non-generalizable survey facilitated by PLANSPONSOR, a member organization.[100] The survey included questions about sponsors' 401(k) plans, such as the amount of assets included in the 401(k) plan and the number of participants in the plan, and the reasons why sponsors decided to offer, or not offer, managed accounts to 401(k) plan participants. To minimize errors arising from differences in how survey questions might be interpreted and to reduce variability in responses that should be qualitatively the same, we conducted pretests with industry representatives. Based on feedback from these pretests, we revised the survey in order to improve question clarity. PLANSPONSOR included a link to our survey in an e-mail that was sent to approximately 60,000 of its subscribers. In addition, PLANSPONSOR promoted the survey eight times over 4 weeks between June 3 and June 28, 2013. A record keeper and one industry association also agreed to forward a link to our survey to their clients and members, respectively.

Fifty-seven sponsors completed our survey, and 25 of them provided contact information, indicating they were willing to speak with us. Forty-eight sponsors indicated that they offer managed accounts to their 401(k) plan participants, and 20 of these sponsors provided us with their contact information. Nine sponsors indicated that they do not offer managed accounts to their 401(k) plan participants, and five of these sponsors provided us with their contact information.

We reviewed the survey responses of those sponsors willing to speak with us and selected sponsors to interview based on the following characteristics:

- Plan size (assets in the plan, number of participants)
- Managed account provider
- Enrollment method (Qualified Default Investment Alternative, or QDIA, vs. opt-in)
- Length of time sponsors have been offering managed accounts

To obtain a variety of perspectives, we selected at least two sponsors with any given characteristic to the extent possible. For instance, we selected several (1) sponsors of varying sizes in terms of the amount of assets included in their 401(k) plans and the number of plan participants; (2) sponsors that use different managed account providers; and (3) sponsors that have been offering managed accounts for more than 5 years. Also, we selected one sponsor that offered managed accounts as a default option. In total, we selected 10 sponsors that offer managed accounts and 2 sponsors that do not offer managed accounts, as shown in table 7.

Sponsor Semi-structured Interviews

We developed semi-structured interview questions to capture information on how sponsors learn about and select managed accounts, how they oversee managed accounts, and the advantages and disadvantages of managed accounts for participants. We developed separate questions for sponsors offering managed accounts and those not offering managed accounts. We shared the interview questions with three sponsors before we began conducting the semi-structured interviews to ensure that the questions were appropriate and understandable. We made no substantive changes to the questions based on this effort. We interviewed 10 sponsors that offer managed accounts and 2 sponsors that do not offer managed accounts. As part of our interview process, we also requested and reviewed relevant documentation from plan sponsors such as quarterly managed account reports from managed account providers or record keepers.

Table 7. Characteristics of Sponsors Selected for GAO Interviews

Sponsors	Total 401(k) plan assets (range)	Number of plan participants (range)	Managed account service provider	Method of offering managed accounts	Length of time sponsor has offered managed accounts (range)
Sponsor 1	$100 million or more	25,000 or more participants	Provider A	Opt-in	Between 2 and 5 years
Sponsor 2	$100 million or more	2,500 to 24,999 participants	Provider A	Opt-in	Less than 2 years
Sponsor 3	$10 million or more but less than $50 million	50 to 499 participants	Provider B	Opt-in	More than 5 years
Sponsor 4	$1 million or more but less than $10 million	Fewer than 50 participants	Provider C	Opt-in	More than 5 years
Sponsor 5	$100 million or more	2,500 to 24,999 participants	Provider A	Opt-in	Between 2 and 5 years
Sponsor 6	$50 million or more but less than $100 million	500 to 2,499 participants	Provider A	Opt-in	More than 5 years
Sponsor 7	$100 million or more	2,500 to 24,999 participants	Provider A	Opt-in	Between 2 and 5 years
Sponsor 8	$100 million or more	25,000 or more participants	Provider A	Opt-in	More than 5 years
Sponsor 9	$50 million or more but less than $100 million	500 to 2,499 participants	Provider D	Opt-in	More than 5 years
Sponsor 10	$50 million or more but less than $100 million	2,500 to 24,999 participants	Provider E	Default	More than 5 years
Sponsor 11	$1 million or more but less than $10 million	Fewer than 50 participants	N/A[a]	N/A[a]	N/A[a]
Sponsor 12	$100 million or more	2,500 to 24,999 participants	N/A[a]	N/A[a]	N/A[a]

Source: GAO analysis of information obtained from interviews with sponsors. | GAO-14-310.

[a]Sponsor does not offer managed accounts.

Participant Survey

As part of our approach for determining the advantages and disadvantages of managed accounts for 401(k) plan participants, we developed a non-generalizable online survey to directly obtain participant perspectives on managed accounts, such as the advantages and disadvantages of managed accounts for 401(k) plan participants and participants' level of satisfaction with their managed account offering. However, we did not receive any completed responses to our survey. The survey was conducted on a rolling basis from August 1, 2013 to February 25, 2014—a link to the survey was distributed at various points in time. We conducted this performance audit from October 2012 through June 2014 in accordance with generally accepted government auditing standards. Those standards require that we plan and perform the audit to obtain sufficient, appropriate evidence to provide a reasonable basis for our findings and conclusions based on our audit objectives. We believe that the evidence obtained provides a reasonable basis for our findings and conclusions based on our audit objectives.

APPENDIX II: METHODOLOGY AND ADDITIONAL RESULTS FROM HYPOTHETICAL SCENARIOS

Participant and Plan Scenarios

To understand the different strategies and structures of managed accounts, we developed and submitted five hypothetical participant scenarios in one hypothetical plan to the eight managed account providers chosen for our case studies.

Table 8. Basic Information for GAO Hypothetical Participant Scenarios Provided to Managed Account Providers

	Scenario 1	Scenario 2	Scenario 3
Current age	30	45	57
Gender	Female	Female	Male
401(k) account balance (for sponsor's plan only)	$10,000	$60,000	$100,000
Initial investments/allocation	70% equity 30% fixed	55% equity 45% fixed	43% equity 57% fixed
Current annual salary/compensation	$36,000	$40,000	$52,000
Current contribution (as a percent of salary) (6 percent employee contribution and 3 percent company match)	9%	9%	9%
State of residence	CA	CA	CA

Source: GAO Analysis of data and information from industry representatives and government statistics. | GAO-14-310.

Table 8 shows basic information provided for the hypothetical participant scenarios 1, 2, and 3.

Table 9 shows the additional personalized information provided to managed account providers for hypothetical participant scenarios 1 and 3.

Table 9. Additional Personalized Information for GAO Hypothetical Participant Scenarios 1 and 3

	Scenario 1A	Scenario 1B	Scenario 3A	Scenario 3B
Expected retirement age	Not provided	62	Not provided	62
Expected age at death[a]	Not provided	86	Not provided	83
Participant-specified risk tolerance (general scale of 1-5, 1 representing lowest risk and 5 representing highest risk)	Not provided	3	Not provided	1
Defined benefit plan expected annual payout	Not provided	None	Not provided	$11,000
Outside assets (including retirement and other savings accounts, etc.)	Not provided	All outside savings, including an IRA from a previous job: $11,500	Not provided	IRA: $69,000
Residential property	Not provided	Current renter	Not provided	Homeowner with mortgage of$85,000
Debt, withdrawal needs, and desired future expenditures	Not provided	Non-mortgage debt of $9,700	Not provided	Non-mortgage debt of $6,000
Spouse/family information	Not provided	Single, no children	Not provided	Wife (age 56, independent contractor, compensation $55,000, expected retirement age 63, $120,000 IRA where riskof investments is 3 of 5 on scale noted above)

Source: GAO Analysis of data and information from industry representatives and government statistics and calculators. | GAO-14-310.

[a] A 2009 report sponsored by The Society of Actuaries and The Actuarial Foundation notes that individuals tend to underestimate their own life expectancy, which may lead managed account providers to underestimate their future financial needs. The study recommends that financial planning programs that allow users to input their own life expectancy, such as those provided by managed account providers, should provide information assisting people in doing so and noting that many people underestimate their life expectancy, which could cause them to underestimate their retirement income needs. The report also found large differences in the treatment of longevity risk (which includes the risk of outliving one's life savings) and inadequate focus on making assets last a lifetime. The report notes that one approach to dealing with longevity risk would be to run scenarios with death occurring at various ages, such as 80, 90, and 95, rather than analyzing a single age at death. See John A. Turner and Hazel A. Witte, *Retirement Planning Software and Post-Retirement Risks* (The Society of Actuaries and The Actuarial Foundation: December 2009).

Table 10 shows some of the hypothetical plan level information we compiled for scenario development.

In addition, to generate hypothetical plan information, we selected 14 hypothetical plan investment options from various asset classes, as shown in table 11. We selected these mutual funds to represent a range of asset classes and based on available information from April 2013 about whether these funds could be found in 401(k) plans.

Table 10. GAO Hypothetical Plan Information

Plan size	$75 million in assets
Matching contributions	On the first 6 percent of pay contributed each year, the company will match 50 cents for each dollar contributed (totalof 3 percent company matching contribution)
Administrative fees	39 basis points per participant, annually
Other plan characteristics	• Managed account offered as an opt-in service only • Plan does not allow hardship withdrawals or loans • Plan does not allow company stock investments by plan participants • All participants pay into Social Security

Source: GAO Analysis of data and information from industry representatives and government statistics. | GAO-14-310.

Table 11. GAO Hypothetical Plan Investment Options

Large company		Expense ratio[a] in basis points (bp)
1	Large blend, index fund	17 bpb
2	Large blend, index fund	9 bp
3	Large growth fund	74 bp
4	Large blend fund	62 bp
Small, midsize company		
5	Mid value fund	79 bp
6	Small growth fund	92 bp
7	Mid growth fund	80 bp
Bond funds		
8	Intermediate-term bond fund	22 bp
9	Inflation-protected bond fund	20 bp
10	Intermediate-term bond fund	43 bp
Foreign and global stock		
11	World stock, large growth fund	79 bp
12	World allocation, large blend fund	107 bp
13	Foreign large blend fund	20 bp
Money market fund		
14	Money market fund – taxable	36 bp

Source: GAO compilation of fund information in January 2014 as reported by Morningstar. | GAO-14-310.

[a] The expense ratio is a fund's operating fees as a percentage of its assets.

[b] Basis points are units equal to one hundredth of a percentage point.

Note: These funds represent actual investment options that could have been available to 401(k) participants as of January 2014, but we have only included a description of each fund based on fund information reported by Morningstar.

We developed the hypothetical scenarios based on data and information from industry representatives—including research firms, other industry groups, and providers—and a calculator and statistics provided by a number of government agencies. To assess the reliability of these data, we considered the reliability and familiarity of the source of the data or information and, when necessary, interviewed representatives of those sources about their methods, internal controls, and results. We determined that the data we used were sufficiently reliable for developing hypothetical participant- and plan-level scenarios.

Provider Responses

We asked all eight managed account providers chosen for our case studies to provide example asset allocations and advice, if practical, for all five hypothetical participant scenarios. Seven of the eight managed account providers completed and returned asset allocations to us for the hypothetical scenarios. Five of the seven providers who sent allocations furnished two allocations for each scenario, but each gave different reasons for doing so. One of the providers furnished two allocations for each scenario because they actively manage participant allocations given changes in market conditions and their allocations could generally range within the two extremes. Another provider furnished two allocations for each scenario assuming different initial holdings because, for that provider's strategy, a person's initial holdings of plan investment options influence the provider's recommended allocations, even though both of these allocations have the same overall risk and return characteristics. In some of the figures presenting results of this work, we have included one or both of these two providers' second allocations. For the other three providers we have chosen to only include one of their asset allocations in the figures presenting the results of this work because they did not pertain to managed account service by itself or they did not include the full services offered by the managed account. We did, however, incorporate the more general understanding we gained from these alternate asset allocations in our report findings.

In addition, a number of providers' systems required that they make certain assumptions about participants outside of the hypothetical scenario information we provided. In these cases, the assumptions they made did differ, sometimes substantially, and this may have affected their asset allocation results. For example, to generate a participant's goal, providers used varying assumptions of a participant's annual salary growth—from 1.5 to 3.5 percent. We did not attempt to categorize or eliminate any inconsistencies in provider strategies, but instead report their results to show the variation that a participant may experience.

Additional Results

As shown in figure 13, the median values of all providers' allocations show a downward trend in asset allocations to equity assets and an upward trend in asset allocations to fixed income and or cash-like assets as participants age.

For each hypothetical participant, we found that providers varied widely in their recommendations of specific investment options, but participants could be similarly allocated to asset classes, such as cash and cash equivalents, equity, and fixed income. For the hypothetical 30-year-old participant, select asset allocations were presented in the report at figure 5, and all allocations to specific investment options are shown in figure 14.

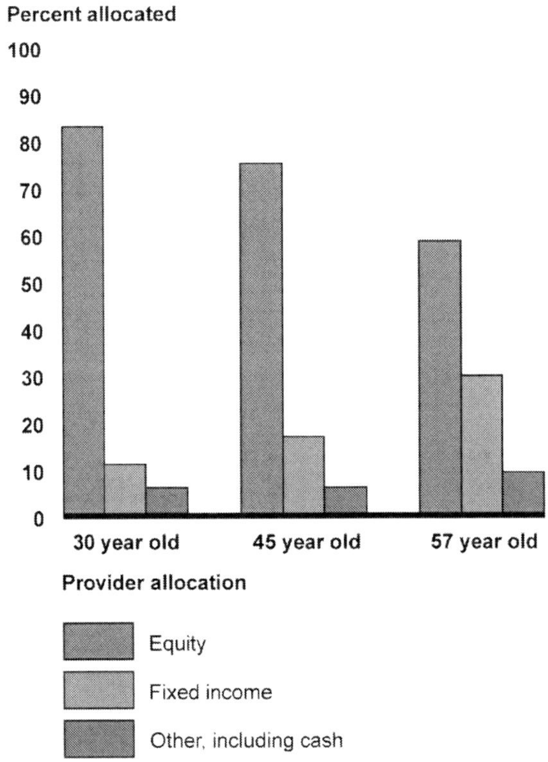

Source: GAO analysis of provider asset allocations. | GAO-14-310.

Note: Since each bar in this figure represents the median result of all providers, the sum of the three bars in each scenario does not add up to 100.

Figure 13. Median Allocations for GAO Hypothetical Participant Scenarios Show a Downward Trend in Allocations to Equity as the Participant Ages.

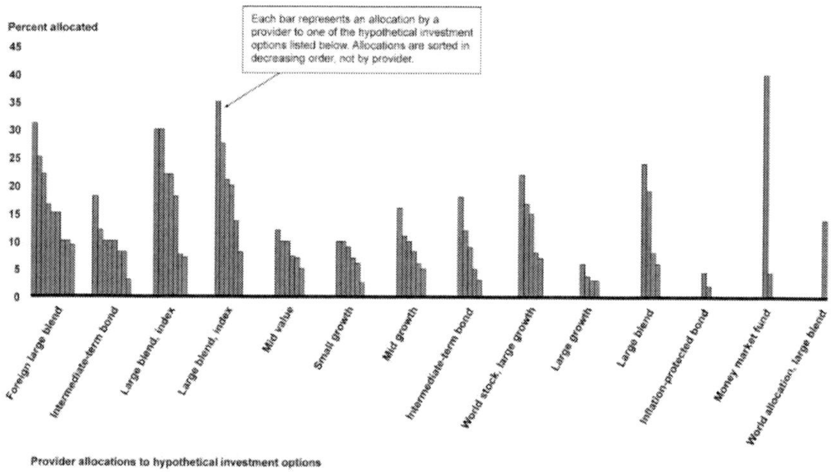

Source: GAO analysis of provider asset allocations. | GAO-14-310.

Note: Seven of the eight managed account providers in our case studies submitted asset allocations for the hypothetical participant scenarios we developed. Some providers submitted multiple allocations given varying assumptions and strategies, and we have included two of those providers' second allocations in this figure. Thus, there are nine allocations to the first hypothetical investment option, "foreign large blend." In addition, some investment options have fewer allocations because providers did not generally allocate portions of the hypothetical participant's account to all investment options. For example, only one provider allocated a portion of the hypothetical participant's account to the last hypothetical investment option, "world allocation, large blend."

Figure 14. Provider Allocations to Hypothetical Investment Options for a Hypothetical 30-year-old Participant.

However, at the asset class level, six of the eight asset allocations for this participant were more aggressive than the initial allocation of 70 percent equity and 30 percent fixed income, while two had more balanced asset allocations as shown in figure 15.

The results were similar for the 45 and 57-year-old hypothetical participants. Starting from an initial asset allocation of 55 percent equity and 45 percent fixed income, providers reported varying asset allocations to investment options for the 45-year-old hypothetical participant, as shown in figure 16, and allocations at the asset class level shown in figure 17.

Starting from initial asset allocation of 43 percent equity and 57 percent fixed income, figure 18 shows variation in allocations to investment options for the 57-year-old hypothetical participant and figure 19 shows variation in allocations at the asset class level.

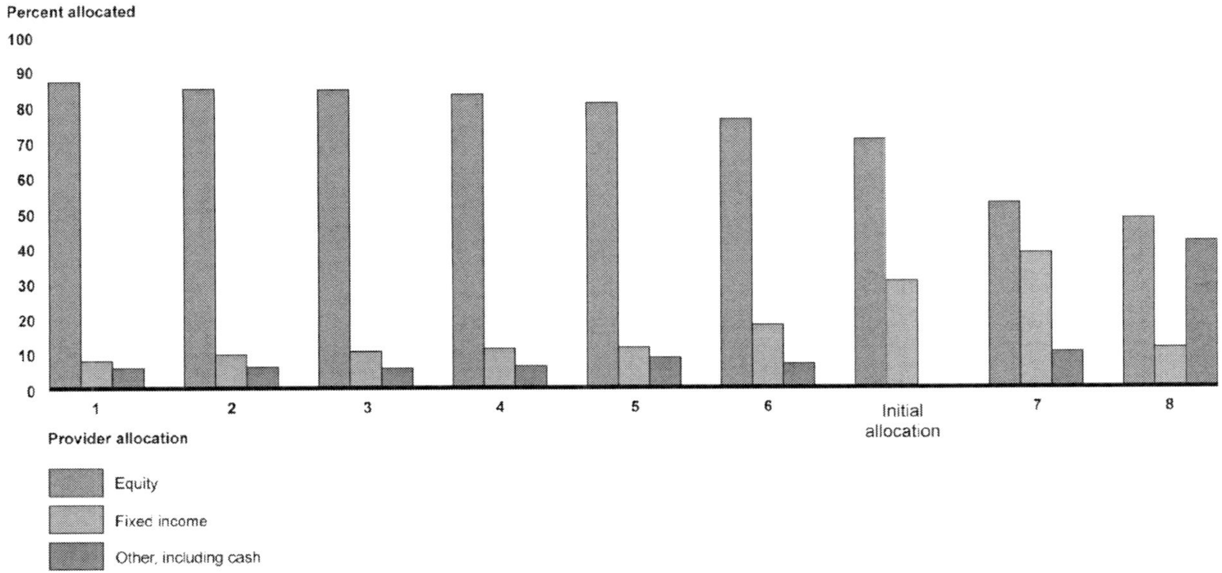

Source: GAO analysis of provider asset allocations. | GAO-14-310.

Note: Seven of the eight managed account providers in our case studies submitted asset allocations for the hypothetical participant scenarios we developed. Some providers submitted multiple allocations given varying assumptions and strategies, and we have included one of those providers' second allocations in this figure.

Figure 15. Provider Allocations to Asset Classes for a Hypothetical 30-year-old Participant.

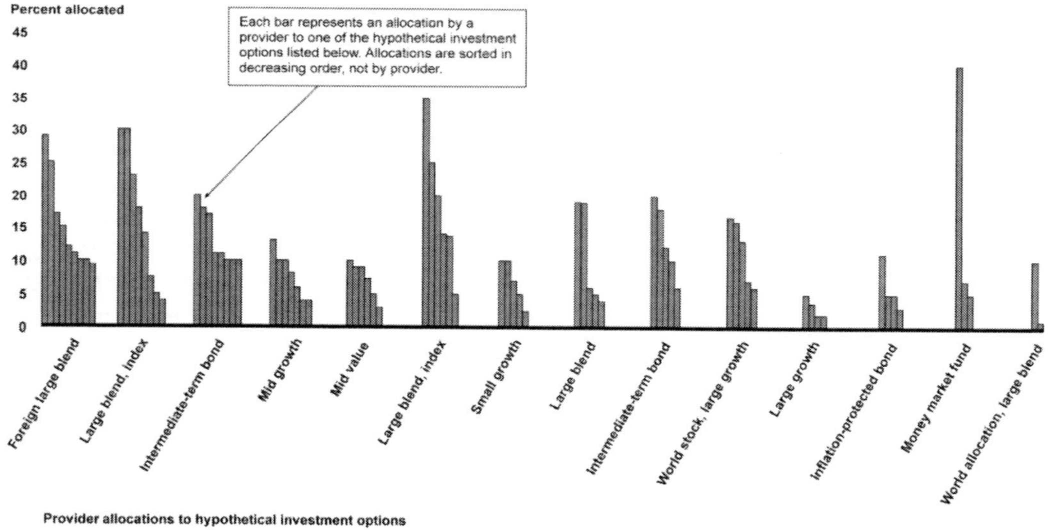

Source: GAO analysis of provider asset allocations. | GAO-14-310.

Note: Seven of the eight managed account providers in our case studies submitted asset allocations for the hypothetical participant scenarios we developed. Some providers submitted multiple allocations given varying assumptions and strategies, and we have included two of those providers' second allocations in this figure. Thus, there are nine allocations to the first hypothetical investment option, "foreign large blend." In addition, some investment options have fewer allocations because providers did not generally allocate portions of the hypothetical participant's account to all investment options. For example, only two providers allocated a portion of the hypothetical participant's account to the 14th investment option, "World allocation, large blend."

Figure 16. Provider Allocations to Hypothetical Investment Options for a Hypothetical 45-year-old Participant.

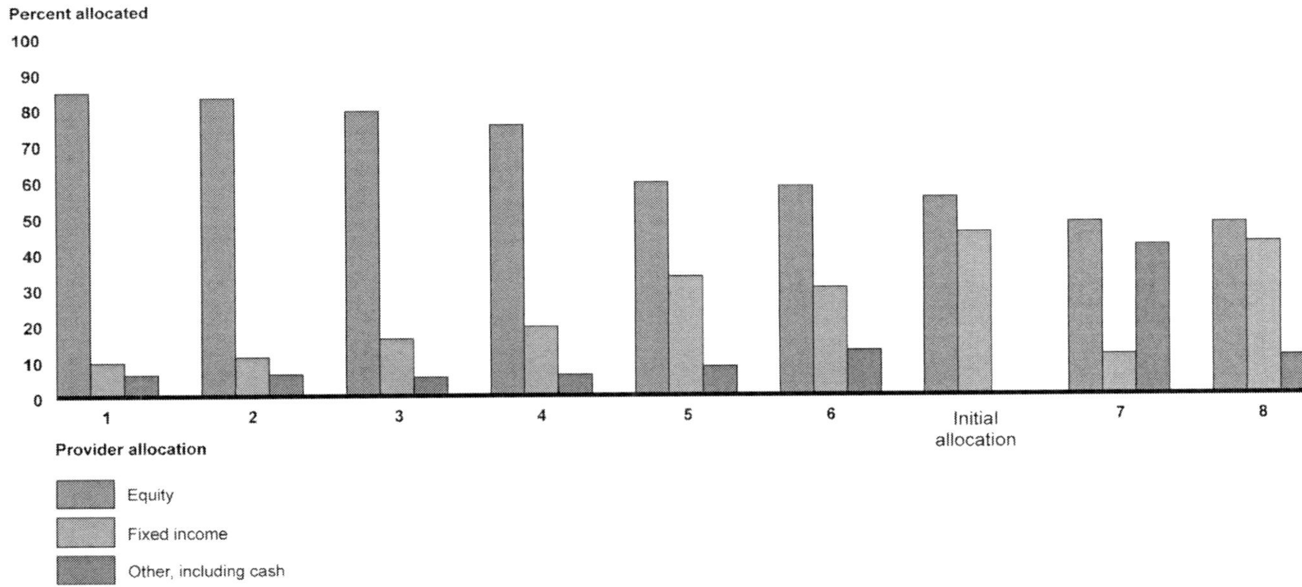

Source: GAO analysis of provider asset allocations. | GAO-14-310.

Note: Seven of the eight managed account providers in our case studies submitted asset allocations for the hypothetical participant scenarios we developed. Some providers submitted multiple allocations given varying assumptions and strategies, and we have included one of those providers' second allocations in this figure.

Figure 17. Provider Allocations to Asset Classes for a Hypothetical 45-year-old Participant.

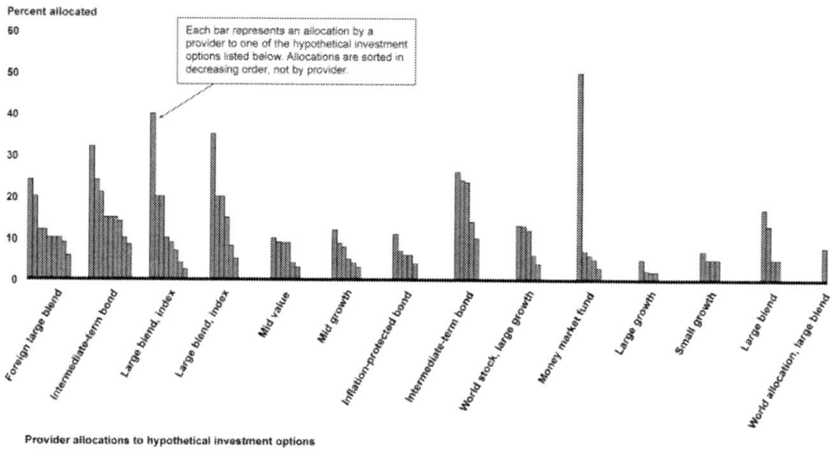

Source: GAO analysis of provider asset allocations. | GAO-14-310.

Note: Seven of the eight managed account providers in our case studies submitted asset allocations for the hypothetical participant scenarios we developed. Some providers submitted multiple allocations given varying assumptions and strategies, and we have included two of those providers' second allocations in this figure. Thus, there are nine allocations to the first hypothetical investment option, "foreign large blend." In addition, some investment options have fewer allocations because providers did not generally allocate portions of the hypothetical participant's account to all investment options. For example, only one provider allocated a portion of the hypothetical participant's account to the 14th investment option, "World allocation, large blend."

Figure 18. Provider Allocations to Hypothetical Investment Options for a Hypothetical 57-year-old Participant.

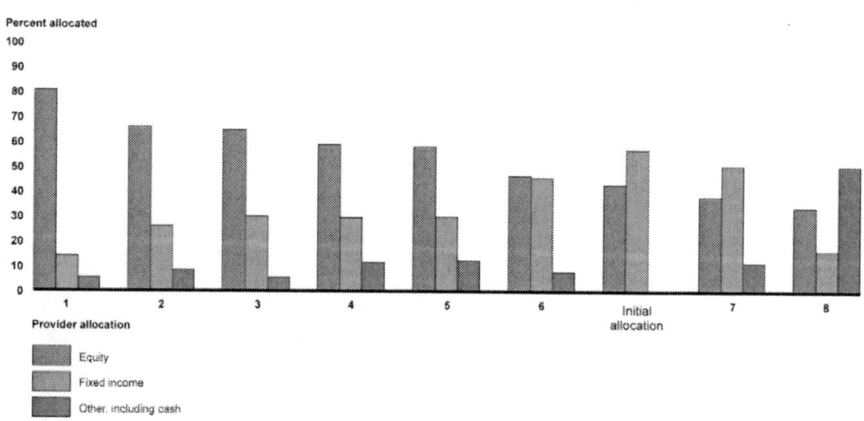

Source: GAO analysis of provider asset allocations. | GAO-14-310.

Note: Seven of the eight managed account providers in our case studies submitted asset allocations for the hypothetical participant scenarios we developed. Some providers submitted multiple allocations given varying assumptions and strategies, and we have included one of those providers' second allocations in this figure.

Figure 19. Provider Allocations to Asset Classes for a Hypothetical 57-year-old Participant.

APPENDIX III: ADDITIONAL PERFORMANCE INFORMATION FROM ONE RECORD KEEPER'S REPORT

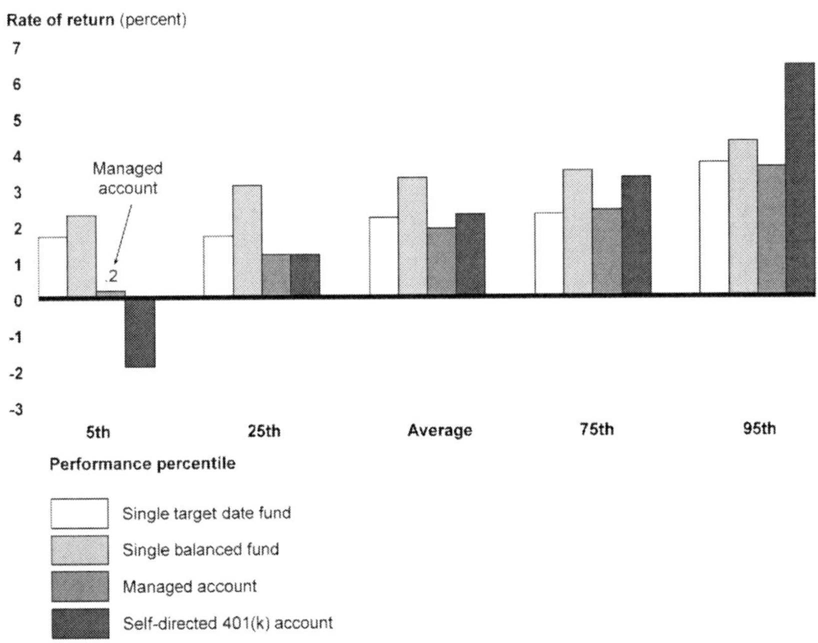

Source: GAO representation of Vanguard returns data. | GAO-14-310.

Note: This record keeper offers managed accounts on its platform and has issued studies on the aggregate performance of professionally managed allocations. Information in these reports is from a limited dataset that can only describe the portfolio performance for this record keeper's defined contribution plan participants with these types of retirement portfolios over a finite period of time. These data are not representative of the portfolio performance of the universe of defined contribution plan participants or for other periods of time. See Vanguard, *Professionally Managed Allocations and the Dispersion of Participant Portfolios* (Valley Forge, PA: August 2013) and Vanguard, *Target Date Funds and the*

Dispersion of Participant Portfolios (Valley Forge, PA: November 2012). These studies examine the effect of professionally managed allocations on participant portfolio construction in defined contribution plans. Professionally managed allocations are participant accounts where 100 percent of the balance is invested by a professional money manager. For these studies, a single target date fund is the most common type of professionally managed allocation, but the category also includes traditional balanced funds and a managed account advisory service. The record keeper's reports also provide performance results for participant-constructed portfolios—portfolios that do not have professionally managed allocations—which we refer to as "self-directed 401(k) accounts." The 5-year returns data include portfolio returns from the recession of 2007-2008. For this reason, the traditional balanced fund had generally higher returns over this period because of their larger fixed income exposure. Return results would likely be different if data from 2007-2008 were not included in the analysis.

Figure 20. Examples of Annualized Rates of Return from One Record Keeper for Different Types of Professionally Managed and Self-directed 401(k) Portfolios, 2007-2012, Net of Additional Fees.

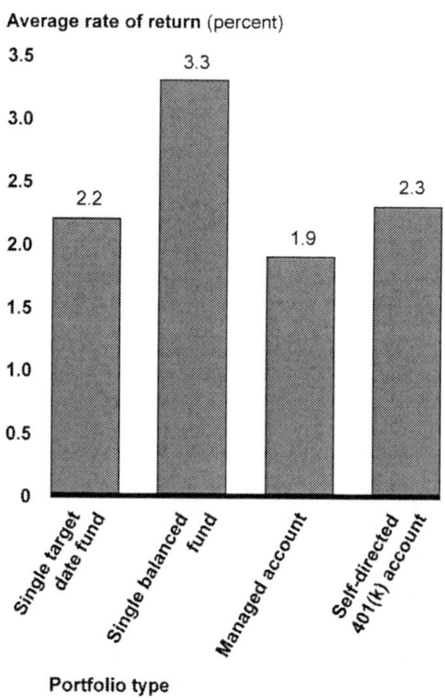

Source: GAO representation of Vanguard returns data. | GAO-14-310.

Note: This record keeper offers managed accounts on its platform and has issued studies on the aggregate performance of professionally managed allocations. Information in these reports is from a limited dataset that can only describe the portfolio performance for this record keeper's defined contribution plan participants with these types of retirement portfolios over a finite period of time. These data are not representative of the portfolio performance of the universe of defined contribution plan participants or for other periods of time. See Vanguard, *Professionally Managed Allocations and the Dispersion of Participant Portfolios* (Valley Forge, PA: August 2013) and Vanguard, *Target Date Funds and the Dispersion of Participant Portfolios* (Valley Forge, PA: November 2012). These studies examine the effect of professionally managed allocations on participant portfolio construction in defined contribution plans. Professionally managed allocations are participant accounts where 100 percent of the balance is invested by a professional money manager. For these studies, a single target date fund is the most common type of professionally managed allocation, but the category also includes traditional balanced funds and a managed account advisory service. The record keeper's reports also provide performance results for participant-constructed portfolios—portfolios that do not have professionally managed allocations—which we refer to as "self-directed 401(k) accounts." The 5-year returns data include portfolio returns from the recession of 2007-2008. For this reason, the traditional balanced fund had generally higher returns over this period because of their larger fixed income exposure. Return results would likely be different if data from 2007-2008 were not included in the analysis.

Figure 21. Average Annualized Rates of Return from One Record Keeper for Different Types of Professionally Managed and Self-directed 401(k) Portfolios, 2007-2012, Net of Additional Fees.

End Notes

[1] A recent Congressional Research Service report noted that relatively few defined contribution plan participants diversify investments across classes of assets or periodically rebalance their accounts to maintain appropriate diversification—two recommendations made by many financial advisers. The report also noted that even if a plan offers a range of low-cost, diversified investment options and offers investment education and investment advice, it is not unusual for some participants to make investment choices that may prove to be unwise in the long run. Congressional Research Service, *401(k) Plans and Retirement Savings: Issues for Congress* (Washington, D.C.: Jan. 7, 2011).

[2] The Plan Sponsor Council of America found in its *49th and 56th Annual Profit Sharing and 401(k) Surveys* that about 25 percent of sponsors offered managed accounts in 2005 but in 2012 this number had grown to about 36 percent.

[3] Service providers are outside entities, such as investment companies, banks, or insurance companies that a plan sponsor hires to provide some of the services necessary to operate the plan. These services include managed accounts, investment management (e.g., selecting and

managing the securities included in a mutual fund), consulting and providing financial advice to the plan sponsor (e.g., selecting vendors for investment options or other services), and recordkeeping (e.g., tracking individual account contributions), among other things.

[4] In defined contribution plans, benefits are based on contributions and the performance of the investments in participants' individual accounts. The predominant type of defined contribution plans are 401(k) plans.

[5] For the purpose of this report, we focused only on arrangements initiated by the plan sponsor for the 401(k) plan—i.e., the 401(k) plan sponsor made a decision to offer the managed account to its participants, either as a default option or on an opt-in basis. By contrast, we did not focus on certain arrangements that could be considered "managed accounts" when the 401(k) plan sponsor was uninvolved. For example, if the plan sponsor offers participants the use of a brokerage window—arrangements under which participants may select investments beyond those designated by the plan, referred to by a variety of names, including brokerage window and self-directed brokerage account—plan participants could independently contract with advisers to manage their retirement savings in the plan. Plan sponsors would usually not be involved in the selection and monitoring of these advisers.

[6] The "Form ADV" is the form used by investment advisers to register with both the SEC and state securities authorities. Among other things, the form requires investment advisers to prepare narrative brochures that provide information such as the types of advisory services offered—including managed accounts in 401(k) plans—the adviser's fee schedule, disciplinary information, and conflicts of interest. This brochure is the primary disclosure document that investment advisers provide to their clients.

[7] PLANSPONSOR is a media and research firm in the retirement benefits industry. According to PLANSPONSOR, it has been the nation's leading authority on retirement and benefits programs since 1993 and is dedicated to helping employers navigate the complex world of retirement plan design and strategy on behalf of their employees.

[8] In 2011, U.S. employers sponsored over 510,000 401(k) plans covering more than 61 million workers with more than $3.1 trillion in plan assets. U.S. Department of Labor, Employee Benefits Security Administration, *Private Pension Plan Bulletin: Abstract of 2011 Form 5500 Annual Reports, Version 1.0* (Washington, D.C.: June 2013). A worker who actively participated in a 401(k) plan may participate in more than one defined contribution plan and also might participate in a defined benefit plan in addition to his or her 401(k) plan. Contributions to the defined contribution plan may also be made by employers.

[9] Stable value funds are designed to preserve the total amount of participants' contributions, or their principal, while also providing steady positive returns.

[10] There is considerable variation in target date fund portfolio construction. See GAO, Defined Contribution Plans: Key Information on Target Date Funds as Default Investments Should Be Provided to Plan Sponsors and Participants. GAO-11-118 (Washington, D.C.: Jan. 31, 2011).

[11] Risk tolerance refers to a participant's ability and willingness to lose some or all of his or her original investment in exchange for greater potential returns. An aggressive investor— one with a high risk tolerance—is more likely to risk losing money in order to get better results by, for example, investing a higher portion of assets in stocks. By comparison, a conservative investor—one with a low risk tolerance—tends to favor investments that will preserve the original investment and thus is more likely to invest a higher portion of assets in lower risk investment options such as bonds.

[12] We use the term "plan sponsors" generally in this report, but in some circumstances the requirements would apply to plan sponsors, plan fiduciaries, or plan administrators, which may be the same entity or different entities, depending on the situation.

[13] Default Investment Alternatives Under Participant Directed Individual Account Plans, 72 Fed. Reg. 60,452 (Oct. 24, 2007) (codified at 29 C.F.R. § 2550.404c-5). The final QDIA

regulation implemented amendments to Title I of ERISA enacted as part of the Pension Protection Act of 2006 (PPA). Pub. L. No. 109–280, § 624, 120 Stat. 780, 980. With the enactment of PPA, section 404(c) of ERISA was amended to provide relief afforded by section 404(c)(1) to fiduciaries that invest participant assets in certain types of default investment alternatives in the absence of participant investment direction. Specifically, section 624(a) of PPA added a new section 404(c)(5) to ERISA, which provides that, for purposes of section 404(c)(1), a participant in an individual account plan shall be treated as exercising control over the assets in the account with respect to the amount of contributions and earnings which, in the absence of an investment election by the participant, are invested by the plan in accordance with regulations prescribed by the Secretary of Labor. Section 624(a) of PPA also directed that such regulations provide guidance on the appropriateness of designating default investments that include a mix of asset classes consistent with capital preservation or long-term capital appreciation, or a blend of both.

[14] 29 C.F.R. § 2550.404c-5(e)(4)(i), (ii), and (iii). DOL also designated principal preservation products for use by plan sponsors, but only within the first 120 days of an individual's participation. 29 C.F.R. § 2550.404c-5(e)(4)(iv) and (v). DOL explained that the 120 day timeframe is intended to provide plans a reasonable amount of time to effectuate the transfer of a participant's assets to another QDIA. *See* 72 Fed. Reg. 60,464.

[15] 29 C.F.R. § 2550.404c-5(b)(1).

[16] 29 C.F.R. § 2550.404c-5(b)(2).

[17] 29 C.F.R. § 2550.404c-5(c)(3) and (d). A worker who is defaulted into a QDIA generally has 90 days to opt out and withdraw any contributions (including the earnings on those contributions). These amounts will not be subject to the extra tax that normally applies to distributions received before age 59½. 26 U.S.C. § 414(w)(2)(B) and 29 C.F.R. § 2550.404c-5(c)(5)(ii).

[18] PLANSPONSOR, *2012 Defined Contribution Survey: Looking to the Stars* (November 2012).

[19] *See generally* 29 C.F.R. § 2550.404a-5. Sponsors are required to furnish participants with plan-related and investment-related fee information annually and with information on administrative and individual expenses actually charged to participants' accounts quarterly on or before the first date a new participant can first direct his or her investments. The purpose of these disclosures is to ensure that participants and beneficiaries have access to plan information to help them make informed decisions about their retirement. For a review of required participant disclosures and notices related to 401(k) plans, see GAO, Private Pensions: Clarity of Required Reports and Disclosures Could Be Improved, GAO-14-92 (Washington D.C.: Nov. 21, 2013).

[20] *See generally* 29 C.F.R. § 2550.404c-5(c)(3) and (d). In addition to providing plan sponsors with relief from certain fiduciary responsibilities, these disclosures help ensure that participants and beneficiaries are in a position to make informed decisions concerning their participation in their employer's plan.

[21] Reasonable Contract or Arrangement Under Section 408(b)(2)—Fee Disclosure, 77 Fed. Reg. 5632 (Feb. 3, 2012)(codified at 29 C.F.R. § 2550.408b-2(c)). In its fact sheet to the 408(b)(2) disclosure final rule, DOL stated that "fundamental to the ability of [sponsors to fulfill] these obligations is obtaining information sufficient to enable them to make informed decisions about an employee benefit plan's services, the costs of such services, and the service providers." See DOL, EBSA, *Fact Sheet, Final Regulation Relating to Service Provider Disclosures Under Section 408(b)(2)* (Washington, D.C.: February 2012).

[22] Some record keepers contract with an intermediary provider that offers the use of multiple managed account providers.

[23] In this report, such record keepers or intermediary providers are not included in the term "managed account provider."

[24] When sponsors default participants into a target date fund the manager of that fund may be responsible for making asset allocation decisions, but the decision to select the fund for the participant is made by the sponsor, not a provider as is the case in a managed account.

[25] *See* 29 U.S.C § 1104(a). Under ERISA, a fiduciary is anyone who has discretionary control or authority over the management or administration of an ERISA-covered plan, such as a 401(k) plan, including the plan's assets, as well as anyone who, for a fee, renders investment advice with respect to a plan. 29 U.S.C. § 1002(21). Plan sponsors and other plan fiduciaries have specific responsibilities under ERISA. In accordance with ERISA and related DOL regulations and guidance, responsibilities of plan sponsors and other fiduciaries may include, but are not limited to: selecting and monitoring any service providers to the plan; reporting plan information to the federal government and to participants; adhering to the plan documents, including any investment policy statements; identifying parties-in-interest to the plan and taking steps to monitor transactions with them; selecting and monitoring investment options the plan will offer and diversifying plan investments; and ensuring that the services provided to their plans are necessary and that the cost of those services is reasonable.

[26] *See* 29 U.S.C. § 1002(21)(A)(ii) and (38). Depending on the facts and circumstances, plan service providers may also play other fiduciary roles under 3(21). *See* 29 U.S.C. § 1002(21)(A)(i) and (iii). Both 3(38) and 3(21) fiduciaries are required to act solely in the interest of participants and beneficiaries.

[27] 29 C.F.R. § 2550.404c-5(e)(4)(iii) and (e)(3)(i), and 29 U.S.C. § 1002(38).

[28] We estimate that these eight providers represented over 95 percent of the managed account industry in defined contribution plans, as measured by assets under management in 2013.

[29] The managed account provider may require that the plan sponsor add investment option(s) in order to offer the managed account. For example, one provider requires sponsors to offer a minimum of 5 asset classes in its 401(k) plan investment options, including U.S. equity, international equity, intermediate-term bonds, small/mid-cap funds, and other bond-type funds (stable value funds, money market funds, or long-term bond funds). Representatives of this provider said that smaller plans were less likely than larger plans to offer investment options in all of these asset classes, and in this case, the provider will consult with the plan sponsor to make the necessary changes. This consulting or advice is separate from the managed account service.

[30] Exchange traded funds are similar to mutual funds in that they offer investors a way to pool their money in a fund that makes investments in stocks, bonds, or other assets and, in return, to receive an interest in an investment pool. However, shares of the exchange traded funds are traded on a national stock exchange and at market prices that may or may not be the same as the net asset value of the shares. Unlike traditional mutual funds, exchange traded funds do not sell individual shares directly to investors, and investors may not redeem individual shares; the funds only issue and redeem their shares in large blocks known as creation units.

[31] Modern portfolio theory is a body of academic and empirical work that focuses on choosing a portfolio, not just its individual parts. Central components include: (1) the concept of diversification—the notion that with a well-chosen group of assets participants may be able to limit their losses and reduce fluctuations of investment returns without sacrificing too much potential gain, and (2) the concept of rebalancing—bringing a participant's portfolio back to an appropriate asset allocation mix—because over time some investments may become misaligned with the participant's investment goals. Rebalancing helps ensure that participant portfolios do not overemphasize one or more asset categories by returning the portfolio to a comfortable level of risk.

[32] The highest return for each level of risk comprises the most efficient mix of investments, or the efficient frontier.

[33] Monte Carlo simulation describes the range of outcomes from a given asset allocation assuming various inputs for expected returns, volatilities, and correlations of investment options in the plan. For more information see Stacy L. Schaus, *Defining Successful Target Date Strategies For Defined Contribution Plans: Putting Participants on the Optimal Glide Path* (Hoboken, NJ: 2010). More information on other techniques, including the Black-Litterman model and resampled mean-variance optimization, can be found in Ibbotson Associates, *Developing Robust Asset Allocations* (Chicago, IL: April 2006)

[34] Active management strategies seek to achieve specific goals and require more hands- on management of the fund by the investment manager than passively managed funds. Experience-based methods for developing asset allocations rely on tradition, experience, or rules of thumb and may be less expensive to implement than efficient frontier methods. Popular experience-based methods include: (1) 60/40 equity/fixed income as a neutral starting point, (2) allocation to fixed income assets increase with participants' risk aversion, (3) allocation to equity assets increase with time horizon, and (4) allocation to equity assets remain at one hundred minus the participant's age. While traditional finance, and modern portfolio theory in general, describes how markets work, some experience- based methods of asset allocation incorporate lessons learned from behavioral finance, a discipline that attempts to describe how investors actually behave. See G. Curtis, "Modern portfolio theory and behavioral finance," *The Journal of Wealth Management*, 7(2) (2004), 16-22.

[35] However, allocations were generally similar across asset classes, such as equity and fixed income. See appendix II for an additional discussion of the methodology and results of this work. We asked all eight providers in our case studies to provide example asset allocations for five hypothetical participant scenarios in one hypothetical plan. Seven of the eight providers submitted asset allocations for the hypothetical participant scenarios we developed and some providers submitted multiple allocations given varying assumptions and strategies.

[36] See appendix II for an additional discussion of the methodology of this work.

[37] See appendix II for an additional discussion of the methodology and results of this work.

[38] We estimate that these eight providers represented over 95 percent of the managed account industry in defined contribution plans, as measured by assets under management in 2013.

[39] In conducting this work, we did not reach independent conclusions about whether or to what extent various entities involved in managed account arrangements are fiduciaries under ERISA because such determinations are generally based on the facts and circumstances of a particular situation. Instead, we report information provided by the entities included in our review.

[40] However, record keepers differ in their approach to this arrangement. Specifically, some record keepers use an intermediary provider that takes on fiduciary responsibility and offers the use of multiple managed account providers, from which plan sponsors select a managed account provider to offer their plan participants. Other record keepers contract with only one managed account provider to obtain access to their managed account software, but every other function to support the managed account is provided by the record keeper.

[41] 3(38) Investment Manager fiduciaries are required to acknowledge in writing that they are fiduciaries with respect to the plan, and in this regard, can be said to "willingly accept" 3(38) fiduciary status. *See* 29 U.S.C. § 1002(38)(C).

[42] This provider requires participants to initially give affirmative consent that they want the provider to initially allocate and annually rebalance their accounts going forward. The provider automatically implements its annual allocations unless participants opt out of the service. According to representatives of the provider, this managed account service has not yet been used by 401(k) plan participants, but one record keeper has agreed to provide this service.

[43] We did not reach any independent conclusions about whether and to what extent this provider is or should be a fiduciary under ERISA.

[44] *See* 29 U.S.C. § 1002(21)(A)(ii) and 29 C.F.R. § 2510.3-21(c).

[45] As noted previously, a 3(38) Investment Manager fiduciary can only be a bank, an insurance company, or an RIA, but there are no similar requirements for 3(21) Investment Adviser fiduciaries, who DOL officials noted could be highly qualified or have limited or no experience.

[46] Plan sponsors, as named fiduciaries of 401(k) plans, are required to act prudently in selecting and monitoring managed account providers that are either 3(38) Investment Manager or 3(21) Investment Adviser fiduciaries. According to DOL officials, if a 3(38) Investment Manager fiduciary is appointed to manage plan assets, the plan trustee—who could be the plan sponsor or some other entity—is relieved from being held responsible for those assets. They further explained that, provided a plan sponsor trustee prudently selects and oversees a 3(38) Investment Manager fiduciary service provider, the sponsor cannot be held responsible for poor investment decisions made by the provider. This protection does not exist for the plan sponsor trustee if a 3(21) Investment Adviser fiduciary is selected.

[47] In QDIA regulations the requirement that a managed account provider be a 3(38) Investment Manager fiduciary is a condition under which a "safe harbor" could be achieved by the plan sponsor. Outside of such a safe harbor, as would be the case with opt-in managed account services, there is currently no similar requirement. DOL officials noted that it is not clear that DOL could require 3(38) Investment Manager fiduciary status outside of such a safe harbor context.

[48] According to the managed account providers in our case studies who offer these additional services, participants receiving asset allocation and savings services from managed account providers while they accumulate retirement assets pay the same fee as participants receiving spend-down services from those managed account providers.

[49] TIPS—derived from their former name, Treasury Inflation-Protected Securities—are inflation-indexed debt issued by the U.S. Treasury. These bonds have principal and coupon payments that are linked to movements in the Consumer Price Index. They are a defensive measure against expectations of inflation, which typically erodes the real yield of conventional bonds. Even if inflation fears are in check, these bonds can benefit when the yields fall on traditional Treasuries. These unique securities act very differently than any other fixed-rate bond, and their volatility can change over time, depending on the level of interest rates.

[50] Although DOL has not addressed this issue, in its 2010 proposal on the definition of fiduciary advice, DOL requested comments on whether and to what extent the final regulation defining fiduciary investment advice should encompass recommendations related to taking a plan distribution, including the costs and benefits associated with extending the regulation to these types of recommendations.

[51] In our previous report on IRA rollovers, we found that participants chose the easiest, most accessible option because they were often unaware of their choices or had to do additional work to gain advantages from the other options. GAO, *401(K) Plans: Labor and IRS Could Improve the Rollover Process for Participants,* GAO-13-30 (Washington D.C.: Mar. 7, 2013).

[52] See Morningstar, *Better Expected Retirement Outcomes with Managed Accounts* (July 15, 2013). In another study of managed accounts, this managed account provider found that its participants who self-directed their 401(k) investments were either too aggressive or too conservative in their asset allocation strategies, and many were significantly underdiversified, with nearly half of the participants in the study having more than 30 percent of their retirement account improperly allocated. See Morningstar, *Making the Case for Managed Accounts* (2011). We did not verify the accuracy of the information provided in this report. Information provided by Morningstar is from a limited dataset and was used

to project future outcomes only for the small set of Morningstar participants enrolled in its advisory service. These data are not representative of the future performance of the universe of defined contribution plan participants.

[53] For additional information on diversification, see U.S. Securities and Exchange Commission, *Beginners' Guide to Asset Allocation, Diversification, and Rebalancing,* accessed on March 17, 2014, http://www.sec.gov/investor/pubs/assetallocation.htm.

[54] See Vanguard, Professionally Managed Allocations and the Dispersion of Participant Portfolios (Valley Forge, PA: August 2013) and Vanguard, Target Date Funds and the Dispersion of Participant Portfolios (Valley Forge, PA: November 2012). These papers examine the portfolio outcomes for Vanguard participants in defined contribution plans who enrolled in a managed account, invested in a target date fund or balanced fund, or self-directed their 401(k) investments from 2007 through 2012 and from 2006 through 2011, respectively. We did not verify the accuracy of the information provided in these reports. Information provided by Vanguard is from a limited dataset that can only describe the portfolio performance for Vanguard defined contribution plan participants with these types of retirement portfolios over a finite period of time. These data are not representative of the portfolio performance of the universe of defined contribution plan participants or for other periods of time.

[55] In addition, managed account providers and sponsors have reported that participants in managed accounts have reduced the percentage of company stock held in their retirement portfolios, which can help to reduce risk associated with investing heavily in a single equity. For example, one sponsor we interviewed said that the managed account it offers participants does not allow investments in company stock and, as a result, the managed account has substantially improved participants' portfolio diversification by decreasing investments in company stock by two-thirds.

[56] See Morningstar, Better Expected Retirement Outcomes with Managed Accounts (July 15, 2013). We did not verify the accuracy of the information provided in this report. Information provided by Morningstar is from a limited dataset and was used to estimate savings and portfolio performance only for small set of Morningstar participants enrolled in its advisory service. These data are not representative of the savings or portfolio performance of the universe of defined contribution plan participants.

[57] This provider presents every participant who enrolls in its managed accounts service with a gap analysis that shows the effect that even a small increase in savings can have on a participant's retirement income. See Morningstar, *Making the Case for Managed Accounts* (2011).

[58] While plan sponsors can contract with their plan administrators or record keepers to offer these types of statements to participants even if they do not offer a managed account, we found that managed account providers consistently offered this feature to participants.

[59] See Vanguard, Professionally Managed Allocations and the Dispersion of Participant *Portfolios* (Valley Forge, PA: August 2013).

[60] Morningstar, Better Expected Retirement Outcomes with Managed Accounts (July 15, 2013).

[61] Vanguard, *Professionally Managed Allocations and the Dispersion of Participant Portfolios* (Valley Forge, PA: August 2013). For additional information obtained from this report, see appendix III.

[62] We found little available data on the performance of managed accounts. For the purpose of this illustration, we used Vanguard's published data on 5-year annualized returns for defined contribution plan participants with either professionally managed allocations or participant-constructed portfolios, which we refer to as a self-directed 401(k) account. The 5-year returns data include portfolio returns from the recession of 2007-2008. Return results would likely be different if data from 2007-2008 were not included in the analysis. Information provided by Vanguard is from a limited dataset that can only describe the portfolio

performance for Vanguard defined contribution plan participants with these types of retirement portfolios over a finite period of time. These data are not representative of the portfolio performance of the universe of defined contribution plan participants or for other periods of time. See Vanguard, Professionally Managed Allocations and the Dispersion of Participant Portfolios (Valley Forge, PA: August 2013) and Vanguard, Target Date Funds and the Dispersion of Participant Portfolios (Valley Forge, PA: November 2012).

[63] The -0.1 percent return represents the 25th percentile in managed account returns performance for the period of 2006-2011. The 2.4 percent return represents the 75th percentile in managed account returns for the period of 2007-2012. See Vanguard, *Professionally Managed Allocations and the Dispersion of Participant Portfolios (*Valley Forge, PA: August 2013) and Vanguard, Target Date Funds and the Dispersion of *Participant Portfolios* (Valley Forge, PA: November 2012).

[64] For the purpose of this illustration, we used fee data reported to us during our case studies of managed account providers. We also used Vanguard's published data on 5- year annualized returns for defined contribution plan participants with either professionally managed allocations or participant-constructed portfolios, which we refer to as a self- directed 401(k) account. The 5-year returns data include portfolio returns from the recession of 2007-2008. Return results would likely be different if data from 2007-2008 were not included in the analysis. Information provided by Vanguard is from a limited dataset that can only describe the portfolio performance for Vanguard defined contribution plan participants with these types of retirement portfolios over a finite period of time. These data are not representative of all possible fees charged to participants for a managed account, the portfolio performance of the universe of defined contribution plan participants, or for other periods of time. See Vanguard, Professionally Managed Allocations and the Dispersion of Participant Portfolios, (Valley Forge, PA; August 2013) and Vanguard, Target Date Funds and the Dispersion of Participant Portfolios, (Valley Forge, PA; November 2012).

[65] The 2.4 percent rate of return represents the 75th percentile for this record keeper's managed account participants for the period of 2007-2012. For the same period, the 75th percentile was 3.3 percent for participants with self-directed 401(k) accounts, 3.5 percent for participants invested in a single balanced fund, and 2.3 percent for participants invested in a single target date fund. See Vanguard, *Professionally Managed Allocations and the Dispersion of Participant Portfolios* (Valley Forge, PA: August 2013)

[66] The -0.1 percent rate of return represents the 25th percentile for this record keeper's managed account participants for the period of 2006-2011. For the same period, the 25th percentile was 0.0 percent for participants with self-directed 401(k) accounts, 2.7 percent for participants invested in a single balanced fund, and 0.3 percent for participants invested in a single target date fund. *See* Vanguard, *Target Date Funds and the* Dispersion of Participant Portfolios (Valley Forge, PA: November 2012).

[67] Participants with 401(k) accounts generally pay investment management fees and other administrative fees to providers or record keepers to maintain their accounts. Investment management fees, which can vary by investment option, are generally charged as a percentage of assets and indirectly charged against participants' accounts because they are deducted directly from investment returns. Administrative fees, on the other hand, can be assessed as an overall percentage of total plan assets regardless of participants' investment choices, in addition to a flat rate for some fixed services, such as printing plan documents. In the latter, the sponsor has the option of passing along some or all of the administrative fees to participants. We previously reported that recordkeeping and administrative fees are often paid by the plan sponsors, but participants bear them in a growing number of plans. GAO, *Private Pensions: Changes Needed to Provide 401(k) Plan Participants and the Department of Labor Better Information on Fees,* GAO-07-21 (Washington, D.C.: Nov. 16, 2006).

[68] Participants generally receive information on the fees they pay to the managed account provider in their plan, but do not receive comparative fee information for other providers. We found few independent sources of comprehensive and consistent information on managed account fees charged by providers that a participant could use to compare fees across providers. PLANSPONSOR publishes an annual Asset Allocation Solutions Buyer's Guide that includes some information on the additional fees certain providers charge for managed accounts. However, the information on fees is not consistent across providers and, in some instances, does not contain information specific enough to allow participants to accurately identify the fee they will have to pay for their individual managed account. Instead, publicly available fee information on managed accounts can usually be found in specific managed account provider SEC filings or sometimes on provider websites, which participants may find confusing or incomplete.

[69] In limited instances, some participants may not pay a fee at all because managed account providers noted that some plan sponsors subsidize or pay the fees charged to participants.

[70] Revenue sharing generally refers to indirect payments made from one service provider to another service provider in connection with services provided to the plan, rather than payments made directly by the plan sponsor for plan services.

[71] For example, one managed account provider may charge a one-time setup fee of $25,000 to cover the costs of setting up a large or particularly complex plan's managed account service, which may have primarily institutional investment options that require additional modeling by the managed account provider. Another provider charges between $6 and $14 per participant in the plan, which is generally paid from plan assets or absorbed into the plan's recordkeeping fees.

[72] The hypothetical participant in our illustration is based on certain reported data, as described in the notes under Figure 10.

[73] *See* Fiduciary Requirements for Disclosure in Participant-Directed Individual Account Plans, 75 Fed. Reg. 64,910 (Oct. 20, 2010) (codified at 29 C.F.R. pt. 2550).

[74] This requirement is referred to as the participant-level disclosure regulation. 29 C.F.R. § 2550.404a-5.

[75] 29 C.F.R. § 2550.404a-5(h)(4).

[76] Specifically, DOL's 2012 field assistance bulletin states that "neither an investment management service nor each individual account it manages should be considered a designated investment alternative, as described under 404a-5(h)(4)." DOL also confirmed in the bulletin that if a plan designates a fiduciary investment manager to allocate the assets in a participant's individual retirement account among the designated investment alternatives available in the plan, neither the investment management service nor the individual account it manages would be considered a designated investment alternative and the disclosure requirements would be satisfied as long as the designated investment manager were identified under 29 C.F.R. § 2550.404a-5(c)(1) and the fees for such services were disclosed under 29 C.F.R. § 2550.404a-5(c)(3). See Field Assistance Bulletin No. 2012-02R.

[77] All participants with a 401(k) account are required to receive fee information from their plan sponsor in a separate disclosure. *See* 29 C.F.R. § 2550.404a-5.

[78] 29 C.F.R. § 2550.404c-5(d)(3).

[79] Target Date Disclosure, 75 Fed. Reg. 73,987 (Nov. 30, 2010)(to be codified at 29 C.F.R. § 2550.404c-5). On June 3, 2014, DOL re-opened the comment period for these proposed amendments through July 3, 2014. See Target Date Disclosure, 79 Fed. Reg. 31,893 (June 3, 2014).

[80] As previously mentioned, in its frequently asked questions for the 404a-5 participant disclosure regulation, DOL clarifies that managed account services may be considered "designated investment managers" and, as such, may not be considered "designated investment alternatives." Because managed accounts are generally a service, some of the investment-

related disclosure requirements in the proposed rule, such as information on the QDIA's investment issuer or the QDIA's objectives, risks, and strategies, may not apply to managed accounts.

[81] However, if the managed account service is limited to the plan's designated investment alternatives, participants would receive the investment-related disclosures for all of the plan's designated investment alternatives, in a comparative chart format as required under the participant-level disclosure regulation at 29 C.F.R. § 2550.404a-5(d).

[82] *See* Fiduciary Requirements for Disclosure in Participant-Directed Individual Account Plans, 75 Fed. Reg. 64,910 (Oct. 20, 2010) (codified at 29 C.F.R. pt. 2550).

[83] A customized benchmark is a blend of more than one broad-based index that reflects the mix of asset classes included in a portfolio. For example, for a portfolio that includes investments in stocks and bonds, a customized benchmark would be composed of a percentage of a broad based stock market performance index as well as a percentage of an appropriate bond index.

[84] The provider has made a generic version of its managed account performance report available to the public on its website—participants and sponsors can see how performance comparisons can be made using the provider's custom benchmarks and can review a description of the benchmarks and other key summary statistics provided on the report.

[85] As previously noted, record keepers maintain recordkeeping systems that are used to track 401(k) plan contributions and returns. They may also offer managed account providers on these systems and play other key roles in the implementation and continued operation of managed accounts. For instance, they provide information to the managed account provider and implement asset allocation changes to participant accounts. Thus, for a sponsor to be able to offer a managed account, the sponsor's record keeper must be able to work effectively with the managed account provider.

[86] Department of Labor, Employee Benefits Security Administration, *Meeting Your Fiduciary Responsibilities* (Washington, D.C.: February 2012).

[87] For example, a large record keeper we interviewed said that it began offering two managed account provider options instead of one because sponsors asked for more options. Similarly, in the past, record keepers have modified their systems to allow for greater target date fund choice pursuant to sponsor requests.

[88] These sponsors had been using an advice service offered by the provider before they selected the provider's managed account service.

[89] Specifically, this provider contracts with several independent RIAs who develop asset allocation model portfolios for participants based on information that the provider collects, such as information regarding plan investment options and any personalized information about participants. The provider standardizes the integration of operation of each investment adviser, so that a single integration with the provider is required, even if the sponsor later decides to switch to another investment adviser that contracts with the provider.

[90] Department of Labor, Employee Benefits Security Administration, *Target Date Retirement Funds - Tips for ERISA Plan Fiduciaries* (Washington, D.C.: February 2013). As previously noted, target date funds are another professionally managed allocation that can be used to invest 401(k) plan participant assets and are also one of the categories of investments that may be eligible as a QDIA pursuant to DOL's regulations.

[91] These reports can include information such as changes in participant savings rates and portfolio risk levels.

[92] One of the providers that furnishes performance information is able to do so even though it develops 101 portfolios for each plan included in its managed account service prior to placing participants into an optimal portfolio.

[93] DOL's service provider disclosure regulations require that some service providers furnish investment-related information, such as performance and benchmarking information

concerning plan designated investment alternatives, that must be disclosed pursuant to the participant-level disclosure regulation. *See* 29 C.F.R. § 2550.408b-2(c)(1)(iv)(E)(3) and 29 C.F.R. § 2550.404a-5(d)(1).

[94] The "Form ADV" is the form used by investment advisers to register with both the Securities and Exchange Commission (SEC) and state securities authorities. The form consists of two parts. Part 1 requires information about the investment adviser's business, ownership, clients, employees, business practices, affiliations, and any disciplinary events of the adviser or its employees. Part 2 requires investment advisers to prepare narrative brochures that provide information such as the types of advisory services offered— including managed accounts in 401(k) plans—the adviser's fee schedule, disciplinary information, and conflicts of interest. The brochure is the primary disclosure document that investment advisers provide to their clients.

[95] Some record keepers and intermediary service providers refer to themselves as "managed account providers" because they make this service available to participants, but they do not ultimately decide how to invest participant contributions. Thus, we excluded most record keepers and intermediary providers from our definition of a managed account provider. Similarly, even though certain other providers, such as target date fund managers, may select an overall asset allocation strategy and investments to fit that strategy for the funds they offer to 401(k) plan participants, these managers also do not ultimately decide how to invest participant accounts.

[96] See Vanguard, Professionally Managed Allocations and the Dispersion of Participant Portfolios (Valley Forge, PA: August 2013) and Vanguard, Target Date Funds and the Dispersion of Participant Portfolios (Valley Forge, PA: November 2012). In Vanguard's reports, return rates for managed accounts, target date funds, balanced funds, and self- directed 401(k) investments are reported at the 95th, 75th, 50th, 25th, and 5th percentile over two different periods, 2006-2011 and 2007-2012, respectively.

[97] Other fee rates that we used in this scenario include 0.2 percent (provider reported), 0.37 percent (provider reported), 0.45 percent (an average of the fees we found), and 0.6 percent (provider reported).

[98] Participant savings are a combination of the amount of salary saved by the participant and the employer match.

[99] The starting account balance of $17,000 is based on the Employee Benefit Research Institute's (EBRI) estimated median 401(k) account balance at year-end 2011; the starting salary of $40,000 is based on the Bureau of Labor Statistics' (BLS) seasonally adjusted median weekly earnings for the third quarter of 2013; the average annual salary increase of 1.75 percent is based on BLS' salary increase estimate for the 12-month period ending September 2013; the savings rate of 9.7 percent is based on the EBRI's estimate of an average employee savings rate of 6.7 percent for 2012 and a standard 3 percent average employer match.

[100] PLANSPONSOR is a media and research firm in the retirement benefits industry. According to PLANSPONSOR, it has been the nation's leading authority on retirement and benefits programs since 1993 and is dedicated to helping employers navigate the complex world of retirement plan design and strategy on behalf of their employees.

In: Managed 401(k) Accounts
Editor: Harold Parker

ISBN: 978-1-63463-592-9

Chapter 2

401(K) PLANS AND RETIREMENT SAVINGS: ISSUES FOR CONGRESS*

John J. Topoleski

SUMMARY

Over the past 25 years, defined contribution (DC) plans—including 401(k) plans—have become the most prevalent form of employer-sponsored retirement plan in the United States. The majority of assets held in these plans are invested in stocks and stock mutual funds, and the decline in the major stock market indices in 2008 greatly reduced the value of many families' retirement savings. The effect of stock market volatility on families' retirement savings is just one issue of concern to Congress with respect to defined contribution retirement plans.

This report describes seven major policy issues with respect to defined contribution plans:

1) *Access to employer-sponsored retirement plans.* In 2007, only 61% of employees in the private sector were offered a retirement plan of any kind at work. Fifty-five percent were offered a DC plan. Only 45% of workers at establishments with fewer than 100 employees were offered a retirement plan of any kind in 2007. Forty-two percent were offered a defined contribution plan.

* This is an edited, reformatted and augmented version of a Congressional Research Service publication, CRS Report for Congress R40707, from www.crs.gov, dated January 7, 2011.

2) *Participation in employer-sponsored plans.* Between 20% and 25% of workers whose employer offers a DC plan do not participate. Workers under age 35 are less likely than older workers to participate.
3) *Contribution rates.* On average, participants in DC plans contributed 6% of pay to the plan in 2007. The median contribution by household heads who participated in a DC plan in 2007 was $3,360. This was just 22% of the maximum allowable contribution of $15,500 in that year.
4) *Investment choices.* At year-end 2007, 78% of all DC plan assets were invested in stocks and stock mutual funds. This ratio varied little by age, indicating that many workers nearing retirement were heavily invested in stocks and risked substantial losses in a market downturn like that in 2008. Investment education and target date funds could help workers make better investment decisions.
5) *Fee disclosure.* Retirement plans contract with service providers to provide investment management, record-keeping, and other services. There can be many service providers, each charging a fee that is ultimately paid by participants in 401(k) plans. The arrangements through which service providers are compensated can be very complicated and fees are often not clearly disclosed.
6) *Leakage from retirement savings.* Pre-retirement withdrawals from retirement accounts are sometimes called "leakages." Current law represents a compromise between limiting leakages from retirement accounts and allowing people to have access to their retirement funds in times of great need. In general, borrowing from a 401(k) plan poses less risk to retirement security than a withdrawal. Pre-retirement withdrawals can have adverse long-term effects on retirement income.
7) *Converting retirement savings into income.* Retirees face many financial risks, including living longer than they expected, investment losses, inflation, and possible large expenses for medical care and long-term care. Annuities can protect retirees from some of these risks, but few retirees purchase them. Developing polices that motivate retirees to convert assets into a reliable source of income will be a continuing challenge for Congress and other policymakers.

New Challenges to a Secure Retirement Income

Over the past 25 years, defined contribution (DC) plans have become the most prevalent form of employer-sponsored retirement plan in the United States. According to the Bureau of Labor Statistics (BLS), 51% of workers in the private sector participated in an employer-sponsored retirement plan of some kind in 2007. Only 20% of all private-sector workers were covered by traditional pensions—also called defined benefit or "DB" plans—whereas 43% participated in 401(k) plans and other DC plans.[1] Twelve percent of workers participated in both types of plan.[2]

One of the key distinctions between a defined benefit plan and a defined contribution plan is that in a DB plan, it is the employer who bears the investment risk. The employer must ensure that the pension plan has sufficient assets to pay the benefits promised to workers and their surviving dependents. In a DC plan, the worker bears the investment risk. The worker's account balance at retirement will depend on how much has been contributed to the plan over the years and on the performance of the assets in which the plan is invested. In a typical 401(k) plan, a worker must decide whether to participate, how much to contribute, how to invest the contributions, what to do with the account if he or she changes jobs, and how to take money out of the account after retiring.

The majority of assets held in DC plans are invested in stocks and stock mutual funds, and as a result, the decline in the major stock market indices in 2008 greatly reduced the value of many families' retirement savings.[3] According to the Federal Reserve Board, assets held in DC plans fell from $3.73 trillion at year-end 2007 to $2.66 trillion at year-end 2008, a decline of 28.7%.[4] The decline would have been even greater if not for ongoing contributions to the plans by workers and employers.

The effect of stock market volatility on families' retirement savings is just one issue of concern to Congress with respect to DC plans. Other issues that have received attention in hearings and through proposed legislation include increasing access to employer-sponsored plans, raising participation and contribution rates, helping participants make better investment choices, requiring clearer disclosure of fees charged to plan participants, preserving retirement savings when workers face economic hardship or change jobs, and promoting life annuities as a source of retirement income.

This report describes these seven major policy issues with respect to DC plans:

- access to employer-sponsored retirement plans,
- participation in employer-sponsored plans,
- contribution rates,
- investment choices,
- fee disclosure,

- leakage from retirement savings, and
- converting retirement savings into income.

ACCESS TO EMPLOYER-SPONSORED RETIREMENT PLANS

According to the National Compensation Survey (NCS), 61% of private-sector workers were employed at establishments that offered one or more retirement plans in 2007. Twenty-one percent worked for employers that offered a DB plan, 55% worked for employers that offered a DC plan, and 15% worked for employers that offered both types of plan.[5] Thus, almost 4 out of 10 workers in the private sector did not have the opportunity to participate in a retirement plan where they worked. Moreover, there is a substantial disparity in sponsorship of retirement plans between large employers and small employers. Workers at establishments with fewer than 100 employees are much less likely to have access to an employer-sponsored retirement plan than are workers at larger establishments. (See Table 1.) Policies that would increase the number of small employers that offer retirement plans could expand access to these plans to include millions more workers.

Plan Sponsorship by Small Employers

Surveys of households and employers illustrate the gap in retirement plan sponsorship between large and small employers. Data collected by the Bureau of the Census indicate that there were 75 million private-sector workers between the ages of 25 and 64 who were employed year-round, full-time in 2007. Thirty million of these workers, or 40%, worked for employers that did not sponsor a retirement plan of any kind. Of these 30 million workers, 19.1 million, or 64%, worked for firms with fewer than 100 employees.[6] Likewise, data from the Department of Labor's 2007 National Compensation Survey show that 78% of workers at establishments with 100 or more employees worked for employers that sponsored retirement plans in 2007, compared with just 45% of workers at establishments with fewer than 100 employees.

Although workers at small establishments are less likely to be offered a retirement plan, when one is offered, they are as likely as employees at larger businesses to participate in the plan. In 2007, for example, 70% of workers at establishments with 100 or more employees were offered a DC plan, and the take-up rate among those offered a DC plan was 76%. At establishments with fewer than 100 employees, 42% of workers were offered a DC plan, and the take-up rate among those offered a DC plan was 79%.[7]

Table 1. Participation in Employer-Sponsored Retirement Plans, 2003 and 2007 (Private-sector workers; in percentages)

Establishment Size	2003	2007	2003	2007	2003	2007
	Offered any plan		Participated in any plan		Take-up rate	
100 or more workers	75	78	65	66	87	85
Under 100 workers	42	45	35	37	83	82
All Workers	57	61	49	51	86	84
	Offered a DB Plan		Participated in DB plan		Take-up rate	
100 or more workers	34	34	33	32	97	94
Under 100 workers	9	9	8	9	89	100
All Workers	20	21	20	20	100	95
	Offered a DC Plan		Participated in DC plan		Take-up rate	
100 or more workers	65	70	51	53	78	76
Under 100 workers	38	42	31	33	82	79
All Workers	51	55	40	43	78	78

Source: U.S. Department of Labor, Bureau of Labor Statistics, National Compensation Survey.

Notes: Data represent 102 million workers in 2003 and 108 million workers in 2007. The take-up rate is the percentage of workers offered a plan who participated in the plan. In 2007, for example, 55% of workers were offered a DC plan and 43% of workers participated in a DC plan. Therefore, the take-up rate was .43/.55 = .78.

Workers at firms with fewer than 100 employees comprised 44% of all private-sector workers in the United States in 2007. If employees at small firms had been offered DC plans at the same rate as employees of larger firms, an additional 11.4 million workers would have had the opportunity to participate in employer-sponsored retirement plans in 2007. If take-up rates among these employees had been the same as at firms that already offered DC plans, an additional 9.0 million workers would have participated in DC plans in 2007.[8]

Defined Contribution Plans for Small Employers

Qualified retirement plans, including 401(k) plans, must comply with the Employee Retirement Income Security Act (ERISA) and the Internal Revenue Code (IRC). Among the requirements for retirement plans to receive favorable tax treatment is that they are prohibited from discriminating in favor of highly-compensated employees (HCEs) in terms of contributions or benefits.[9] This assures that rank and file employees as well as owners and managers benefit from the tax breaks that Congress has granted to tax-qualified retirement plans. The nondiscrimination tests compare the participation rates and plan contributions for HCEs to those of other employees.[10] In a small firm, relatively modest changes in employee participation or contributions can make the difference between the plan passing or failing the nondiscrimination test. If the plan fails, some of the contributions made by HCEs must be returned to them and included in their taxable income for the year. A plan that fails the nondiscrimination test also can lose its tax-qualified status, but this penalty is applied only in rare circumstances.

To encourage more employers, especially small employers, to sponsor retirement plans, Congress has authorized several kinds of defined contribution plans that are exempt from some administrative requirements that otherwise would apply. In some cases, plans that adopt certain characteristics that favor rank-and-file workers are exempt from nondiscrimination testing.

"Safe-Harbor" 401(k) Plans

In 1996, Congress authorized a "safe-harbor" 401(k) plan that exempts the plan sponsor from the annual nondiscrimination tests in exchange for the employer agreeing to make contributions to the plan. In a safe-harbor 401(k), the employer must either contribute an amount equal to 3% of pay on behalf of each *eligible* employee or match the first 3% of salary deferrals of each *participating* employee on a dollar-for-dollar basis and match the next 2% of employee deferrals at 50 cents per dollar.[11] Any firm with one or more employees can establish a safe-harbor 401(k).

Savings Incentive Match Plans for Employees of Small Employers (SIMPLE)

The Small Business Job Protection Act of 1996 (P.L. 104-188) authorized the Savings Incentive Match Plan for Employees of Small Employers (SIMPLE). In exchange for mandatory employer contributions, the plan is exempt from the nondiscrimination tests. An employer that sponsors a

SIMPLE must either contribute an amount equal to 2% of pay on behalf of every *eligible* employee or match 100% of the first 3% of each *participating* employee's contributions to the plan. The maximum allowable employee contribution to a SIMPLE is $11,500 per year in 2010 and 2011. Participants aged 50 and older can make additional contributions of up to $2,500 to a SIMPLE plan. SIMPLE plans can be established only by employers with fewer than 100 employees that do not already have retirement plans.

Simplified Employee Pension (SEP)

In the Revenue Act of 1978 (P.L. 95-600), Congress authorized a defined contribution plan called the Simplified Employee Pension (SEP) for firms that do not already sponsor a retirement plan. Only the employer can make contributions to a SEP, and the employer can decide from year to year whether to contribute to the plan. Employer contributions must be made on behalf of all eligible employees, and the contributions must be the same percentage of pay for all eligible employees. Contributions cannot exceed an amount equal to 25% of pay up to a maximum of $49,000 in each year 2010 and 2011 (indexed to inflation). Participants are fully and immediately vested in the employer's contributions to the plan. Any firm with one or more employees can establish a SEP.

Plan Sponsorship Remains Low among Small Employers

Despite the availability of the SEP, SIMPLE, and safe-harbor 401(k), there has been relatively little growth in retirement plan sponsorship among small firms over the past 20 years. According to the Bureau of Labor Statistics, 36% of employees at small private-sector establishments participated in an employer-sponsored retirement plan of some kind in 1990.[12] By 2007, the participation rate in all types of retirement plans among employees at small private-sector establishments had increased by just one percentage point to 37%.[13]

One reason that small firms are less likely than large firms to offer retirement plans is that small employers are much more likely than large employers to go out of business in any given year. For example, over the six years from 2000 through 2005, an average of 10.2% of firms with fewer than 20 employees went out of business each year. Among firms with 20 to 99 employees, an average of 4.6% of firms went out of business annually, whereas among firms with 500 or more employees, an average of 2.3% of firms went out of business each year.[14] Because small firms face relatively greater uncertainty about their survival from year to year, their owners are less likely to offer a retirement plan to their employees.

Policy Issue: Automatic IRAs

Because small employers are less likely to sponsor retirement plans for their employees, policy analysts have continued to search for ways to help employees of these firms save for retirement. One proposal that has received considerable attention is to promote the adoption of payroll deduction IRAs by employers who do not sponsor retirement plans. Some such proposals would require employers above a certain size who do not sponsor a retirement plan to allow employees to contribute to an IRA through payroll deduction.[15]

Payroll deduction IRAs are not subject to the Employee Retirement Income Security Act. Small business owners who are concerned about the administrative burden of complying with ERISA might be willing to set up a payroll deduction IRA for their employees. Although some small business owners who already have retirement plans for their employees might drop these plans in favor of payroll deduction IRAs, many will not because it would reduce their opportunity to save for retirement on a tax-deferred basis. In 2011, the annual contribution limit for an IRA is $5,000 whereas the maximum employee contribution to a 401(k) is $16,500. A small business owner who sponsors and participates in a 401(k) plan can save more for retirement on a tax-deferred basis than he or she could save in an IRA. If IRA contribution limits were the same as 401(k) contribution limits, small business owners would be more likely to drop 401(k) plans for IRAs.

One possible area of concern with respect to payroll deduction IRAs is that because they are not subject to ERISA, workers who save through these plans do not have the same rights and protections as participants in 401(k) plans. The participation and vesting requirements of ERISA are not relevant to payroll deduction IRAs, but ERISA has rigorous fiduciary standards that provide important protections to plan participants. Not all of these protections extend to IRAs.

PARTICIPATION IN EMPLOYER-SPONSORED RETIREMENT PLANS

Even when an employer offers a retirement plan, not all employees choose to participate. In 2007, about 75% of employees whose employer sponsored a 401(k) plan participated in the plan, and about 78% of eligible employees participated in DC plans of all types.[16] Participation in a 401(k) plan usually requires the employee to elect to contribute to the plan. Although some 401(k) plans now automatically enroll eligible employees, almost two-thirds of DC plans continue to require employees to elect to participate.[17]

Sponsorship Rates and Take-up Rates

Participation rates are affected both by access to retirement plans and take-up rates among employees who are offered a plan. The take-up rate is the percentage of employees offered a plan who choose to participate. For example, only 32% of workers under the age of 35 participated in DC plans in 2007.[18] (See Table 2.) Although this was due in part to the relatively low percentage of these workers whose employers sponsored plans, another important factor was the low take-up rate among younger workers who were offered a plan. Only 70% of workers under age 35 whose employer sponsored a DC plan participated in the plan in 2007. In contrast, the take-up rate among workers aged 35 to 44 was 82%, and the take-up rate among workers aged 45 to 54 was 83%.[19]

In contrast to the lower participation rate of younger workers compared with older workers, participation rates among employees of small firms are lower than those of employees of larger firms mainly because a smaller proportion of workers at small firms are employed by firms that sponsor retirement plans. Among employees who are offered a retirement plan, take-up rates are similar for employees of small firms and large firms. The data presented in Table 2 show that in 2007, only 9% of workers employed at firms with fewer than 20 employees participated in a DC plan, compared with 35% of workers at firms with 20 to 99 employees, 46% of those at firms with 100 to 499 employees, and 57% of those at firms with 500 or more employees. However, only 12% of workers at firms with fewer than 20 employees were *offered* a DC plan, compared with 46% of those at firms with 20 to 99 employees, 59% of those at firms with 100 to 499 employees, and 70% of workers at firms with 500 or more employees. Take-up rates were similar among employees at small firms and large firms. The take-up rate in 2007 among employees at firms with fewer than 20 employees was 77%, whereas the take-up rates among workers at firms with 20 to 99 employees and firms with 100 to 499 employees were 75% and 78%, respectively. The take-up rate at firms with 500 or more employees was slightly higher (81%).[20]

Table 2. Participation in Defined Contribution Plans: 2004 and 2007 (Working household heads and spouses under age 65)

	Offered a DC Plan		Participated in DC Plan		Take-up Rate	
	2004	**2007**	**2004**	**2007**	**2004**	**2007**
Age						
55 to 64	49.9	48.2	43.1	40.2	86.5	83.5
45 to 54	50.1	54.6	40.0	45.3	79.9	83.0
35 to 44	48.4	49.0	38.2	40.2	79.1	82.1
Under 35	42.4	45.6	28.6	31.8	67.5	69.7
Size of Firm						
500+ employees	67.7	70.4	52.8	57.0	78.0	80.9
100-499 employees	56.1	58.7	41.4	45.8	73.7	78.0
20-99 employees	43.6	46.3	34.3	34.9	78.8	75.4
Under 20 employees	14.9	11.9	11.9	9.2	80.1	76.9
Education						
College graduate	58.6	59.5	49.1	50.6	83.8	85.0
Some college	46.3	50.5	35.1	39.3	75.7	77.9
High school less	37.8	39.4	26.5	28.6	70.2	72.7
Household Income						
Top quartile	60.9	61.5	53.0	53.9	87.1	87.5
Second quartile	52.6	54.5	41.4	45.6	78.7	83.8
Third quartile	43.5	46.3	31.1	33.6	71.4	72.5
Bottom quartile	25.8	29.7	13.9	17.0	54.1	57.4
Total	**47.3**	**49.4**	**36.7**	**39.2**	**77.5**	**79.3**

Source: CRS analysis of the Federal Reserve Board's 2004 and 2007 *Survey of Consumer Finances*.

Notes: Data represent 112 million workers in 2004 and 115 million workers in 2007. Education is the highest level of education completed by the head of household. The take-up rate is the percentage of workers offered a plan who participated in the plan. In 2007, for example, 49.4% of workers were offered a DC plan and 39.2% of workers participated in a DC plan. Therefore, the take-up rate was .392/.494 = .793.

Access to employer-sponsored retirement plans and participation in plans also differ between better-educated and less-educated workers and between workers in higher-income and lower-income households. Only 39% of workers in households in which the household head had a high school education or less worked for an employer that sponsored a DC plan in 2007, compared with 60% of workers in households in which the household head was a college graduate. The take-up rate among the less-educated group was 73%, compared with 85% for those in the better-educated group. Similarly, only 30% of workers in households in the bottom quartile of household income worked for an employer that sponsored a DC plan in 2007, compared with 62% of workers in households in the top income quartile. The take-up rate among workers in the bottom income quartile was just 57%, compared with 88% among workers in the top income quartile.

These results imply that policies intended to raise participation in retirement plans should be designed with the situation of the target population in mind. Efforts to increase plan participation among younger workers should be focused on the low take-up rate among young employees who are offered a plan, perhaps by encouraging firms to adopt automatic enrollment or to provide more education for workers about the importance of saving for retirement. Policies designed to raise participation among employees of small firms will need to target the low sponsorship rate among small employers, which may require finding new ways to make offering a retirement plan less burdensome and costly to small employers. Less-educated workers may need more guidance, perhaps in the form of investment education and investment advice, than better-educated workers. Workers in lower-income households, who may be hesitant to opt into a 401(k) plan that will reduce take-home pay, may be more receptive to plans that devote a portion of future pay increases to the retirement plan.

Policy Issue: The Retirement Savings Tax Credit

Congress has established tax incentives to encourage employers to sponsor retirement plans and employees to participate in these plans. Employer contributions to qualified plans are a tax-deductible business expense, and neither contributions—whether made by the employer or the employee—nor the investment earnings on those contributions are taxed as income to the employee until they are withdrawn from the plan.[21]

Because higher-earning workers pay higher marginal tax rates than lower-earning workers, the tax deduction for contributing to a retirement plan is worth more to a worker in a higher tax bracket than it is to a worker in a lower tax bracket. For a worker with a marginal income tax rate of 35%, contributing $1 to a 401(k) plan costs just 65 cents after taking the tax deduction into account. For a worker with a marginal income tax rate of 20%, contributing $1 to a 401(k) plan costs 80 cents on an after-tax basis. Moreover, both economic theory and empirical evidence suggest that the propensity to save rises with income. Because higher-earners would save much of their income even without tax incentives to do so, a substantial share of the tax revenue lost through the deduction for contributions to retirement plans does not result in a net increase in national saving. Consequently, some economists have suggested that the tax incentives for retirement saving are "upside down." Most of these tax breaks are enjoyed by higher-wage workers who would be likely to save part of their income even without a tax deduction, rather than by low-wage workers who might respond to an effective tax incentive with new saving.

One strategy for increasing contributions to retirement plans would be to provide tax incentives that are targeted to low- and middle-income workers. To provide an additional incentive for lower-income workers to contribute to retirement savings plans, Congress in 2001 authorized a new retirement savings tax credit, sometimes called the "saver's credit." In 2011, single taxpayers with adjusted gross income (AGI) up to $17,000 are eligible for a credit of 50% on qualified retirement contributions up to $2,000. For single filers with AGI of $17,001 to $18,250, the credit is 20%, and for single filers with AGI of $18,251 to $28,250, the credit is 10%. Married couples filing jointly with AGI up to $34,000 are eligible for a credit of 50% on qualified retirement contributions up to $2,000. For married couples with AGI of $34,001 to $36,500, the credit is 20%, and for married couples with AGI of $36,501 to $56,500, the credit is 10%.

The saver's credit is now claimed on about 5 million tax returns each year.[22] The maximum credit is $1,000. The average credit in 2007 was $167. Although the saver's credit provides an incentive for lower-income workers to save for retirement, its effect has been limited because the credit is non-refundable and phases out steeply over a range of income that is relatively low. A nonrefundable credit reduces taxes owed by the amount of the credit. However, if the individual or family owes no income tax after having taken the exemptions and deductions for which they are eligible, a nonrefundable credit has no value.[23] This is the case for many households with modest earnings who might benefit from the saver's credit if the credit were refundable.[24]

H.R. 1961 of the 111th Congress would have increased the rate of the tax credit for retirement savings contributions, mad the credit refundable, and required the credit to be paid into retirement accounts. The income limit for the maximum credit of 50% of contributions would have been increased to an adjusted gross income of $32,500 for individuals and $65,000 for couples. The credit would have phased out between $32,500 and $42,500 for individuals and between $65,000 and $85,000 for married couples filing jointly. The bill would have set the maximum amount of an employee contribution that is eligible for the credit at $500 for an individual and $1,000 for a couple. The contribution limits would have increased by $100 and $200, respectively, each year until 2020. After that time, the limits would have been indexed to the rate of inflation.

CONTRIBUTIONS TO RETIREMENT SAVINGS PLANS

If an employee elects to participate in a 401(k) plan, the next important decision he or she must make is how much to contribute to the plan. Studies have shown that employees are more likely to contribute to a plan if it provides matching contributions, and the amount that an employee contributes to a plan can be influenced by the formula for the matching contribution.[25] About two-thirds of all 401(k) plans offered an employer matching contribution in 2007.[26] The most common matching formula was 50% of the first 6% of pay contributed by the employee, for a total employer contribution equal to 3% of employee pay.

The maximum permissible annual contribution to a retirement plan is limited by federal law, but very few workers contribute amounts near the annual legal maximum.[27] Many employees contribute only enough to receive the full amount of the employer matching contribution. Those who elect not to contribute to a plan that offers a match, or who contribute less than the amount necessary to receive the full match, are in effect choosing to reduce their own compensation below the maximum available to them.[28]

In defined contribution plans, the benefit available to the worker at retirement is the amount in his or her account. The account balance depends on the amount that the employer and employee have contributed to the plan, the investment gains or losses on those contributions, and the fees charged to participants. Research has shown that, historically, the most important factors affecting workers' retirement account balances at retirement are the number of years over which they have contributed and the amounts that they contributed each year to their retirement plans.[29] Consequently, persuading workers to save more and to begin saving earlier are two of the most effective ways of increasing workers' income in retirement.

Household Contributions to DC Plans in 2007

Table 3 shows households' monthly contributions to DC plans in 2007 both in dollars and as a percentage of household earnings. The top panel of the table shows contributions categorized by the age of the household head, the middle panel shows contributions categorized by household income, and the bottom panel shows contributions by all households that contributed to a DC plan.

In 2007, the median monthly contribution to defined contribution plans by households in which at least one worker aged 25 to 64 participated in a DC plan was $290. This is equivalent to $3,480 on an annual basis.[30] As a percentage of household earnings, the median contribution by households in which one or more workers participated in a DC plan was 5.1% of earnings. Twenty-five percent of households that contributed to a DC plan in 2007 contributed $660 or more per month, and 25% contributed $130 per month or less. As a percentage of earnings, 25% of households participating in DC plans contributed 8.3% of earnings or more to the plan in 2007, and 25% of participating households contributed 2.9% of earnings or less to the plan.

Household Contributions by Age of Household Head

Households headed by persons under age 35 contribute less to DC plans, both in dollars and as a percentage of household earnings, than households headed by individuals aged 35 and older. In 2007, the median monthly contribution to DC plans by households headed by persons under age 35 in which at least one worker participated in a plan was $190. Among households headed by persons aged 35 to 44, the median monthly contribution was $310, and among households headed by persons aged 45 to 44, the median monthly contribution was $368. The median monthly DC plan contribution among households headed by persons aged 55 to 64 was $330 in 2007.

As a percentage of total household earnings, the median monthly contribution to DC plans by households headed by persons under age 35 in which at least one worker participated in a plan was 4.2% of earnings. The median contribution among households headed by persons aged 35 to 44 was 5.2% of earnings. Among both households headed by persons aged 45 to 54 and households headed by persons aged 55 to 64, the median contribution to DC plans in 2007 was 5.7% of household earnings.

Household Contributions by Household Income

As one might expect, household contributions to DC plans vary substantially by household income. This is likely to be the case both because higher-income households have more disposable income to save and also because, as was discussed earlier, the tax deduction for retirement savings is more valuable to higher-income households than to lower-income households. In addition, higher-income households are more likely than lower-income households to have more than one worker contributing to a DC plan.

In 2007, the median monthly contribution to DC plans among households in the top income quartile in which one or more workers participated in a plan was $750. Among households in the bottom income quartile in which one or more workers participated in a DC plan, the median monthly contribution to DC plans was $100. As a percentage of income, the median contribution among households in the top income quartile was 6.6% of household earnings, whereas among households in the bottom income quartile, the median contribution was 4.3% of household earnings.[31]

Table 3. Monthly Household Contributions to Defined Contribution Plans in 2007

	Monthly Contributions in Dollars	**Percentage of Household Earnings**
Age of Householder		
55 to 64		
75th percentile of contributions	$790	9.9%
50th percentile of contributions	330	5.7
25th percentile of contributions	133	3.1
45 to 54		
75th percentile of contributions	810	8.5
50th percentile of contributions	368	5.7
25th percentile of contributions	158	3.1
35 to 44		
75th percentile of contributions	750	8.6
50th percentile of contributions	310	5.2
25th percentile of contributions	150	2.9

Table 3. (Continued)

	Monthly Contributions in Dollars	Percentage of Household Earnings
Under 35		
75th percentile of contributions	360	6.0
50th percentile of contributions	190	4.2
25th percentile of contributions	87	2.5
Household Income		
Top income quartile		
75th percentile of contributions	1,292	10.0
50th percentile of contributions	750	6.6
25th percentile of contributions	380	3.6
Second income quartile		
75th percentile of contributions	500	8.2
50th percentile of contributions	303	5.1
25th percentile of contributions	170	3.0
Third income quartile		
75th percentile of contributions	250	6.1
50th percentile of contributions	160	4.4
25th percentile of contributions	90	2.5
Bottom income quartile		
75th percentile of contributions	160	6.2
50th percentile of contributions	100	4.3
25th percentile of contributions	50	2.5
All Contributing Households		
75th percentile of contributions	660	8.3
50th percentile of contributions	290	5.1
25th percentile of contributions	130	2.9

Source: CRS analysis of the Federal Reserve Board's 2007 Survey of Consumer Finances.

Notes: Households are grouped by total income, including earnings and all other income. Contributions are reported as a percentage of total household earnings. Among households in which there was a worker under age 65 in 2007, those with income of $100,780 or more were in the top income quartile and those with income under $33,940 were in the bottom income quartile. Median income for these households was $59,650.

Policy Issue: Automatic Contribution Escalation

Employer matching contributions have been shown to raise participation rates in 401(k) plans. Many employees, however, contribute just enough to receive the full employer match. Employer matching contributions usually phase out at relatively low employee contribution rates. Matching contributions on employee salary deferrals of more than 6% of pay are relatively uncommon. Consequently, employer matching contributions are not as effective at raising employee contribution rates over time as they are at inducing employees to start contributing to the plan. Just as automatic enrollment has proven to be an effective means of raising participation rates in 401(k) plans, automatic contribution escalation can raise contribution rates.

The Pension Protection Act of 2006 sought to encourage employers to adopt automatic enrollment as a feature of their retirement plans by granting an exemption to certain regulations to plans that include a "qualified automatic contribution arrangement."[32] One of the features that a qualified automatic contribution arrangement must include is automatic escalation of employee contributions. Employee deferrals must be equal to specific percentages of pay unless the employee elects a different percentage. The minimum required deferral amount is 3% of pay in the employee's first year of participation, 4% in the second year, 5% in the third year, and 6% in the fourth and later years. The automatic deferral cannot exceed 10% of pay, but participants can elect a higher deferral rate, provided their total deferrals for the year do not exceed the annual limit under I.R.C. § 402(g). In 2011, this limit is $16,500.

A qualified automatic contribution arrangement also must include employer contributions. The employer contribution can be either a non-elective contribution equal to at least 3% of pay for all employees or a matching contribution equal to 100% of the first 1% of salary deferred and 50% of deferrals from 1% of pay to 6% of pay. Other matching formulas are permitted if they result in matching contributions that are at least equal to the amount provided under the prescribed matching formula, do not increase as the employee's rate of deferral increases, and do not apply to deferrals in excess of 6% of pay.

In 2007, the median employee salary deferral into employer-sponsored defined contribution plans was 6% of pay; however, 25% of workers who contributed to a DC plan deferred 3.9% of pay or less. Qualified automatic contribution arrangements that include automatic contribution escalation could raise employee contribution rates for a substantial percentage of participants. Employees could elect not to participate or to lower their contributions. The experience of most plans with automatic enrollment has been that the majority of participants who are automatically enrolled continue to participate. There is less evidence on the long-term effects of automatic contribution escalation on employee contributions because not as many plans have yet adopted automatic escalation.

INVESTMENT CHOICES AND INVESTMENT RISK

A worker who has elected to participate in a 401(k) plan and has decided how much to contribute to the plan usually also must decide how to invest these contributions. More than 90% of 401(k) plans allow employees to direct the investment of their contributions, and three-fourths of plans allow employees to direct the investment of the employer's contributions.[33] In order for a plan sponsor to be relieved of liability for investment losses in a participant-directed retirement plan, participants must be given a choice of at least three investment alternatives, each of which must have different risk and return characteristics.[34] Most plans offer participants more than the minimum number of investment choices required by law. In 2007, the average 401(k) plan offered participants 18 investment options.[35] The investment options most commonly offered were actively managed U.S. stock funds (77% of plans), actively managed international stock funds (73%), indexed U.S. stock funds (70%), and actively managed U.S. bond funds (64%).[36]

Participants in 401(k) plans bear the risk of investment losses. An individual's retirement account might suffer investment losses because the particular stocks, bonds, or other assets in which he or she has chosen to invest decline in value. Diversification can reduce the risk associated with investing in specific assets because declines in the value of some assets may be fully or partially offset by gains in the value of other assets. Stock and bond mutual funds, for example, help protect individuals from investment risk by purchasing securities from many companies in a variety of industries. In a stock mutual fund, investment losses from companies that are performing poorly may be offset by investment gains from companies that are performing well.

A broader form of investment risk is *market risk*, which is the possibility of an overall decline in a broad class of assets, such as stocks. Even a well-diversified portfolio of stocks, for example, will not protect the value of an individual's retirement account from depreciating if stock values fall across the board, as they did in 2008. This is why most investment advisors recommend diversification not only within a class of assets—by buying broadly diversified stock mutual funds instead of individual stocks, for example—but also diversification across asset classes. Bond prices have historically been less volatile than stock prices, and there have been long periods when returns on stocks and bonds have not been closely correlated. Life-cycle funds and target date funds diversify across classes of assets by buying shares in stock mutual funds, bond funds, and sometimes other investments as well.

Although most financial advisors recommend diversifying investments across classes of assets and periodically re-balancing accounts to maintain appropriate diversification, relatively few plan participants put this advice into practice. The assets of DC plans are heavily invested in stocks and stock mutual funds. At year-end 2007, 78% of all DC plan assets were invested in stocks and stock mutual funds. Investment in stocks and stock mutual funds varied little by age, indicating that many workers nearing retirement were heavily invested in stocks, and risked substantial losses in a market downturn like that in 2008. According to the 2007 Survey of Consumer Finances, nearly 30% of DC plan participants between the ages of 35 and 54 had 100% of their account balance invested in stocks in 2007. Twenty-eight percent of participants aged 55 to 64 had their entire account balance invested in stocks and stock mutual funds. (See Figure 1.)

Because many plan participants lack basic financial literacy, policy analysts have suggested that plans should take steps to help participants make better investment choices or adopt plans that automatically allocate contributions among various classes of investments. Investment education and target date funds are two approaches to achieving asset diversification in DC plans.

Policy Issue: Investment Education and Investment Advice

To make informed decisions about how much to save for retirement and how to invest these savings, plan participants need to understand certain basic principles of finance. For example, an individual who understands the risk-

and-return characteristics of stocks and bonds will be better able to balance the risk of investment losses with the expected rate of return from each kind of investment compared to someone who lacks this understanding. Not everyone understands investment risk, however, and many people make decisions about their investments that are not well-informed. Some 401(k) plan sponsors have attempted to help employees make better investment decisions by providing investment education, offering investment advice, and adding "life-cycle funds" or "target date funds" to their plans.

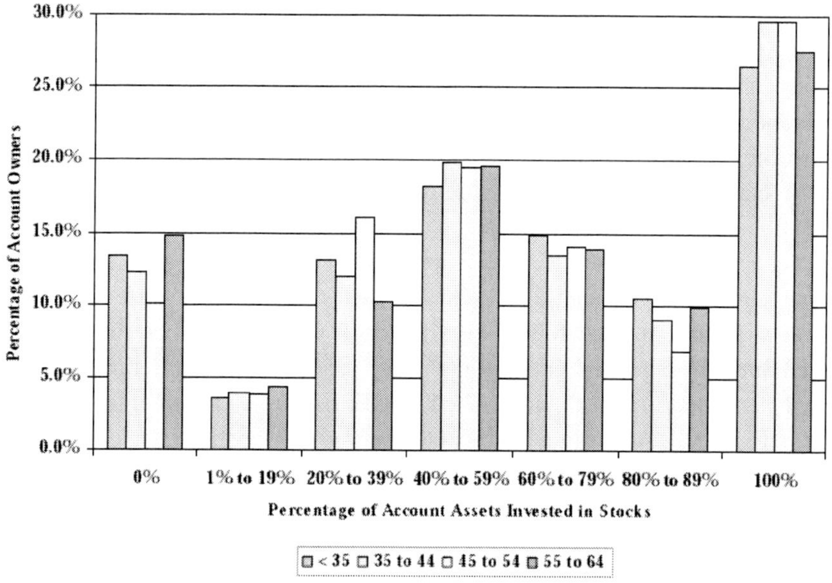

Source: CRS analysis of the Federal Reserve Board's 2007 Survey of Consumer Finances.

Notes: Household heads under age 65 with a defined contribution plan.

Figure 1. Percentage of Defined Contribution Plan Assets Invested in Stocks, 2007; (By age of account owner).

Investment Education

According to Hewitt Associates, more than 90% of all 401(k) plans offer some form of investment education. Typically, investment education is offered through enrollment kits, seminars and workshops, and internet sites. Investment education helps plan participants understand the importance of saving for retirement. It typically focuses on educating individuals about basic tenets of finance, such as the effects of compound interest and the difference between stocks and bonds. Employees who understand how investment gains compound over time are more likely to start contributing to the plan, to continue to contribute to the plan, and to raise their contributions as their earnings rise over time. Participants who understand that the higher expected rate of return on stocks compared to bonds comes at the cost of greater price volatility will be better able to balance their tolerance for risk with their desire for higher returns when choosing investments. Even with more investment education, some employees will choose not to participate in retirement savings plans because they prefer higher current income to higher income in retirement. For workers who discount future income heavily, changing their default participation status to automatic enrollment may be more effective than investment education.

Investment Advice

Investment education consists mainly of giving plan participants general information about the basic principles of finance that they need to be informed investors. Investment advice, on the other hand, is tailored to the individual and often involves recommending specific investments. Some plan sponsors have been reluctant to offer investment advice both because of the cost of paying professional advisors and concerns about possible legal liability for investment losses incurred by plan participants. Almost half (49%) of all 401(k) plans offered investment advice to plan participants in 2007, up from 35% in 2000.[37]

Even if a plan offers a range of low-cost, diversified investment options and offers investment education and investment advice, it is not unusual for some participants to make investment choices that may prove to be unwise in the long run. For example, some participants invest too much of their retirement savings in the stock of their employers. This exposes them to the risk of losing their retirement savings as well as their jobs if the firm goes out of business. Others invest too conservatively while they are young—putting most of their contributions into low-yielding money market funds, for example—even though their longer investment horizon would suggest that they could take on more risk. Sound investment advice can help plan participants avoid these common mistakes.

Under ERISA, providing investment advice is a fiduciary act. A plan sponsor could be held liable for investment losses incurred by a participant who follows investment advice offered by a plan or its agent. The Pension Protection Act of 2006 (PPA) amended ERISA to allow plan sponsors who follow certain procedures to provide investment advice without being held liable for investment losses of participants who act on the advice.[38] In general, to be permissible under the provisions of the PPA, the advice must be provided for a fee rather than a commission, or it must be based on a computer model that meets requirements set forth in statute and regulations. The advisors must disclose their fee arrangements to plan participants and inform them of their affiliations with investments they recommend and with the developer of the computer model. The model on which the advice is based must "operate in a manner that is not biased in favor of investments offered by the fiduciary adviser or a person with a material affiliation or contractual relationship with the fiduciary adviser."[39]

Investment Advice Regulations and Legislation

On January 21, 2009, the Department of Labor (DOL) published a final regulation on the investment advice provisions of the PPA. On March 19, the department delayed the effective date of the regulation for 60 days, pending further review and receipt of additional public comments. On May, 21, 2009, the department announced that the regulation would not be implemented until November 18, 2009. On November 20, 2008, DOL announced that it was withdrawing the final rule. [40]

The investment advice provisions of the PPA allow investment advice to be provided to plan participants by individuals with a financial interest in the investments that they recommend, provided that they disclose this information to plan participants. On April 23, 2009, Representative Robert Andrews introduced H.R. 1988, the Conflicted Investment Advice Prohibition Act of 2009. This bill would allow investment advice to be provided to plan participants only by independent investment advisers who are registered under the Investment Advisers Act of 1940 and who meet certain other qualifying requirements. The bill would prohibit advisers from managing any investments in which any of the assets of the plan are invested, and it would prohibit plans in which individuals direct the investment of their accounts from contracting with investment advisers who are not independent advisers. Independent advisers would be required to provide participants with documentation of the historic rates of return of investment options available to the plan, and to notify participants that the investment adviser is acting as a fiduciary of the plan.

Policy Issue: Life-cycle Funds and Target Date Funds

Even if a plan participant understands the basic principles of finance, he or she may have neither the time nor the inclination to monitor and manage a retirement account. Because many plan participants lack either the aptitude, interest, or time to manage their retirement accounts, plan sponsors have begun to add "life-cycle funds" or "target date funds" to their 401(k) plans. These plans are designed to allocate the participant's investments between stocks and bonds in a way that takes into account his or her risk tolerance and expected date of retirement. Although these funds have proved popular with participants and have won the approval of many investment professionals, the sharp downturn in stock prices in 2008 showed that they are not without problems. Many target-date funds for people expecting to retire in 2010 or 2011 were heavily invested in stocks and lost 25% to 30% of their value in 2008.

Life-cycle funds and target date funds are similar. Many financial analysts consider target date funds to be a subset of the category of funds called life-cycle funds. A life-cycle fund is a mutual fund in which the allocation of assets among stocks, bonds, and cash-equivalents (money market funds, for example) is automatically adjusted during the course of the participant's working life. As the participant nears retirement age, the investment allocation is shifted away from higher-risk investments, such as stocks, and moves toward lower-risk investments, such as bonds and cash equivalents. A target-date fund is a life-cycle fund designed to achieve a particular (generally conservative) mix of assets at a specific date in the future, which is usually the year when the participant expects to retire.

Although life-cycle funds and target date funds are typically designed with the intent of achieving more rapid growth in the early years of the participant's career and greater stability of asset values in the later years, they can contain any mix of stocks, bonds, and cash. There are no industry standards or federal regulations that specify what allocation of assets is required for a life-cycle fund or a target date fund that is intended for plan participants of a given age or with a particular investment time horizon. Currently, less than 5% of DC plan assets are invested in life-cycle funds. Analysts expect this percentage to rise over the next 10 years because the Pension Protection Act allows companies to use life-cycle funds as the default investment option for employees who are automatically enrolled in a 401(k) plan and who do not select an investment fund for their 401(k) contributions.[41]

Allocation of assets among stocks, bonds, and cash-equivalents varies greatly among target date funds with the same target retirement date. A recent study by Morningstar, Inc. found that among target-date 2010 funds that were at least three years old, stock allocations ranged from 14% of assets to 63% of assets. In December 2008, the average 2010 fund had more than 45% of its assets invested in stocks. Fund performance also varied greatly during the bear market of 2008. The S&P Target Date 2010 Index Fund, a benchmark of fund performance, fell 17% in 2008. The fund holds 60% of its assets in bonds and other fixed-income securities and 40% in equities. In comparison, the Deutsche Bank DWS Target 2010 Fund fell just 4% in 2008, whereas Oppenheimer's Transition 2010 fund fell 41%. In January, 2009, the Thrift Savings Plan's "L2010 Fund" for federal employees who plan to retire in 2010 held 70% of its assets in bonds and 30% in stocks. Shares of the L2010 Fund fell 10.5% in 2008.

In a letter sent to Secretary of Labor Hilda Solis in February 2009, Senator Herb Kohl, chairman of the Senate Special Committee on Aging, urged the Secretary to "immediately commence a review of target date funds and begin work on regulations to protect plan participants."[42] In her reply to Senator Kohl on March 26, Secretary Solis stated that the Department of Labor would, in coordination with the Securities and Exchange Commission, begin a review of target date funds to determine if these funds should be subject to further federal regulation.[43]

FEES AND FEE DISCLOSURE

Another issue that has concerned Congress is the effect of fees on retirement account balances. Retirement plans contract with service providers to provide investment management, record-keeping, and other services. There can be many service providers, each charging a fee that is ultimately paid by plan participants. The arrangements through which service providers are compensated can be very complicated. Because the structure of 401(k) fees is opaque to most plan participants, it is very difficult for them to judge whether they are receiving services at a price they would be willing to pay in a more transparent market transaction.

The Administrative Structure of 401(k) Plans

Figure 2 illustrates the administrative structure of a typical 401(k) plan. Plan participants have individual accounts to which the employees, the employer, or both contribute. As the plan sponsor, the employer arranges for one or more third parties to provide various services for the plan. Services include recording transactions, arranging for loans, cashing out departing employees' accounts, and contracting with the funds into which participants can direct their contributions. Employers can purchase services separately from several service providers or they might purchase two or more services from a single service provider. Services may be priced individually or purchased in a bundled arrangement. In a bundled arrangement, several services are offered to the plan for a single fee. The service provider sometimes contracts out the provision of these services to one or more third parties.

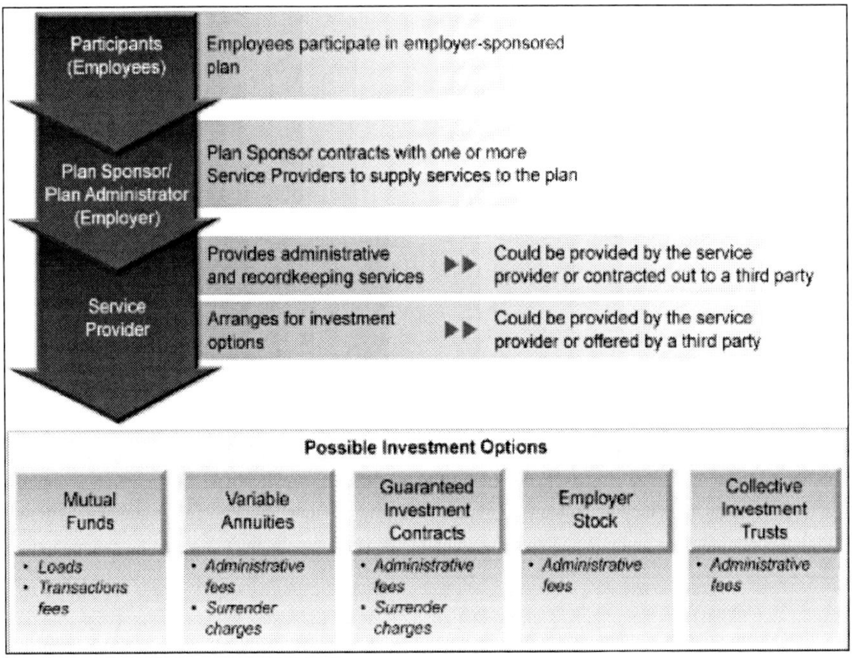

Source: Congressional Research Service.

Figure 2. The Structure of a Typical Defined Contribution Plan.

Fees vary from plan to plan. They are affected by the amounts and kinds of services offered to plan participants and also by the size of the plan. As a percentage of plan assets, fees are negatively correlated with the number of plan participants and the average account balance. In general, the greater the number of plan participants and the larger the average account balance, the lower the fees will be as a percentage of plan assets. A recent survey conducted by Deloitte Consulting for the Investment Company Institute looked at fees in plans ranging in size from those with fewer than 100 participants and less than $1 million in total assets to plans with more than 10,000 participants and assets of more than $500 million.[44] The study looked at fees for administration, recordkeeping, and investment management, which were combined into a single "all-in" fee, expressed as a percentage of plan assets. The median fee for all plans in the survey was 0.72% of plan assets, or approximately $350 for an account with the median balance of plans in the survey, which was $48,500. The study found that 10% of plans had total fees of 0.35% of assets or less and that 10% of plans had total fees of 1.72% of assets or more.

Policy Issue: Requiring Clearer Disclosure of Fees

The firms that provide record-keeping, investment management, and other services to 401(k) plans charge fees for these services, and many of these fees are passed on to plan participants. Fees for some services are charged for each transaction, while others are charged as a flat fee per account per year, and still others—such as investment management—are typically charged as a percentage of total plan assets. Small differences in fees can yield large differences in account balances at retirement, especially in the case of yearly or recurring fees.[45] For example, after 20 years, an initial $20,000 account balance earning 7% yearly would be worth about $70,000 if fees were equal to 0.5% of plan assets each year. The account would have a balance of about $58,000, or 17% less, if fees amounted to 1.5% per year. Over the course of 30 years, a participant in a plan charging fees equal to 1.5% of assets would pay almost $33,000 more in fees than he or she would have paid if the annual fees were 0.5% of assets.[46]

Section 404(a) of ERISA states that plan sponsors are responsible for "defraying reasonable expenses of administering the plan." This has been interpreted by the Department of Labor as imposing a duty on plan sponsors to assure that expenses—including fees—are reasonable. Plan sponsors are not required to minimize fees, but they are required to make sure that plan fees are "reasonable." This standard allows for wide variation in fees across plans. Although sponsors of DC plans are required by law to assure that fees are reasonable, they do not have the same financial incentive to keep fees low as do the sponsors of DB plans. In a DC plan, many fees are passed through to the plan participants, while in a DB plan most fees are paid by the plan sponsor.[47] If plan participants were better-informed about the fees that they pay and the services they receive in return for those fees, they could question plan sponsors about fees that they believe to be unreasonable. Therefore, policies that increase the transparency of fee arrangements could result in participants paying lower fees.

Plans are required by law to disclose some of the fees that plan participants pay. However, the information is not always easily accessible or easily understood by the average participant. On July 16, 2010, DOL issued final regulations requiring greater disclosure of fees.[48]

Members of Congress have been developing legislation that would require greater disclosure of fees to participants. Several bills were introduced in the 111th Congress to increase fee disclosure.

On February 10, 2009, Senator Tom Harkin introduced S. 401, the Defined Contribution Fee Disclosure Act. On April 21, 2009, Representative George Miller introduced H.R. 1984, the 401(k) Fair Disclosure for Retirement Security Act. On June 24, the House Education and Labor Committee ordered the 401(k) Fair Disclosure and Pension Security Act reported to the House. The bill reported by the committee was numbered H.R. 2989. This bill combined H.R. 1984 with H.R. 1988, the Conflicted Investment Advice Prohibition Act, which was introduced by Representative Robert Andrews. On June 9, 2009, Representative Richard Neal introduced H.R. 2779, the Defined Contribution Plan Fee Transparency Act, which was referred to the Committee on Ways and Means.

Leakage from Retirement Savings Plans

The tax incentives that Congress has authorized for retirement savings accounts are designed to assure that the money workers have set aside for retirement remains in the account until they are near retirement age. In recognition of needs that may arise over the course of an individual's life, Congress has allowed certain exceptions to the general restriction on access to these accounts before retirement. Each exception, however justifiable on its own merits, increases the danger that workers will reduce their retirement savings before they have reached retirement.

Pre-retirement withdrawals from retirement accounts are sometimes described as "leakages" from the pool of retirement savings. Congress has used a combination of regulation and taxation to limit and discourage pre-retirement access to money in retirement accounts, but it has not completely prohibited pre-retirement access to these accounts because this access is important to many plan participants. Research has shown that workers are less likely to put money into a retirement account if they believe that the money will be inaccessible in the event of emergency. Consequently, current law represents a compromise between limiting leakages from retirement accounts and allowing people to have access to their retirement funds in times of great need.

Leakages from retirement plans can take a variety of forms, including "hardship" withdrawals from the plan prior to retirement, borrowing against plan assets, and cashing out plan assets upon separation from employment.

Hardship Distributions

The tax code permits 401(k) plans to make distributions available "upon hardship of the employee."[49] Although the Internal Revenue Code (IRC) allows plans to make these distributions available, it does not require them to do so. Federal regulations specify that a hardship distribution can be made only on account of "an immediate and heavy financial need of the employee" and cannot exceed the amount of the employee's previous elective contributions.[50] Qualifying expenses include medical care for the participant or family members, the purchase of a principal residence, college tuition and education expenses, expenses to prevent eviction or foreclosure on a principal residence, and funeral expenses.

A hardship distribution must be limited to the amount needed to meet the employee's immediate financial need plus any taxes that will result from the distribution. Plan participants are prohibited from making contributions to a plan for a period of six months after a hardship distribution, and consequently they forego any employer match on contributions during that time. Hardship distributions are always subject to ordinary income taxes, and unless the distribution is used for a purpose specifically designated in law, the distribution will be subject to a 10% early withdrawal tax penalty unless the plan participant is over age 591/2.[51]

Borrowing from Retirement Plans

The IRC allows participants in employer-sponsored retirement plans to borrow from their accounts, but plans are not required to allow such loans. A loan cannot exceed the greater of $10,000 or 50% of the participant's vested benefit in the plan, up to a maximum of $50,000. Most loans from retirements plans must be paid back within five years, although loans used to purchase a home can be repaid over 15 years. If repayment ceases, the IRS will treat the full amount of the loan as a distribution from the plan, and it will be subject to income tax and possibly to an early distribution penalty. Most plans require employees who separate from the employer before the loan is repaid to repay the balance immediately or the loan will be treated as a taxable distribution from the plan.[52]

For the plan participant, borrowing from a 401(k) plan is usually preferable to taking a hardship withdrawal. With a loan, the account balance is not permanently reduced because the loan will be repaid into the account, generally within five years. Unlike a hardship distribution, after which employee contributions must be suspended for six months, the participant can continue to contribute to the plan while the loan is outstanding. Also unlike hardship distributions, loans are not subject to income taxes or the early withdrawal penalty if repayments continue on schedule.

According to the Federal Reserve Board's Survey of Consumer Finances, 9.5% of households in which the householder or spouse participated in a DC plan had one or more plan loans outstanding in 2007. The mean balance of all loans from DC plans was $6,683 and the median loan balance was $5,000. Ten percent of households with loans from DC plans had outstanding loan balances of $15,000 or more and 10% of households had loan balances of $1,000 or less.

Leakages When Switching Jobs

Leakages from retirement savings can occur when workers change jobs.[53] A participant in a retirement plan usually has several options to choose from when leaving a job. He or she can

- keep the account in the former employer's plan;
- roll over the account into the new employer's retirement plan;

- roll over the account into an Individual Retirement Account (IRA); or
- receive the account balance directly as a distribution from the plan.[54]

Policy Issue: Preserving Retirement Savings

Congress has amended the IRC several times to encourage workers who change jobs to leave their accrued retirement benefit in the former employer's plan or to roll over the account into an IRA or another qualified retirement plan. For example:

- Section 72(t) of the IRC imposes a 10% tax in addition to ordinary income taxes on distributions from retirement plans received before age 591/2 that are not rolled over into an IRA or another tax-qualified plan within 60 days.[55]
- The Unemployment Compensation Amendments of 1992 (P.L. 102-318) require employers to give departing employees the option to transfer a distribution directly to an IRA or to another employer's plan. If the participant instead chooses to receive the distribution, the employer is required to withhold 20%, which is applied to any taxes due on the distribution.[56]
- IRC §411(a)(11) allows a plan sponsor to distribute to a departing employee his or her accrued benefit under a retirement plan without the participant's consent only if the present value of the benefit is less than $5,000.[57] The Economic Growth and Tax Relief Reconciliation Act of 2001 (P.L. 107-16) requires that if the present value of the distribution is at least $1,000, the plan sponsor must deposit the distribution into an IRA unless otherwise instructed by the participant.

In developing policies to prevent leakages from retirement savings, Congress has attempted to promote the preservation of savings until workers retire while recognizing that they may have to take money from their accounts in times of financial hardship. An example of how these goals have been balanced is the treatment of distributions when a worker leaves a job in which he or she participated in a retirement plan. In this situation, Congress has sought to *encourage* recipients to roll over pre-retirement distributions from retirement plans, but it has not *required* such distributions to be rolled over into an IRA or another retirement plan. Current law allows accrued benefits worth less than $5,000 to be cashed out automatically, but it requires the plan participant to agree in writing to a distribution of more than $5,000. The law allows workers to take cash distributions from plans when they leave a job, but it requires 20% to be withheld against taxes owed, and it places an additional 10% tax on amounts that are not rolled over into another retirement account within 60 days of the distribution.

Current law on pre-retirement distributions represents a compromise between competing goals. Stricter limits on access to retirement savings prior to retirement could lower participation or contributions. Research has shown that participation in plans that do not permit plan loans or hardship distributions is lower than in plans that allow these kinds of access to funds held by the plan. Allowing easier pre-retirement access to retirement accounts could lead to more leakages from the plans, depleted account balances, and poorer retirements for many. Moreover, to the extent that retirement accounts could be freely tapped before retirement, they would not be retirement accounts at all, but merely tax-deferred general-purpose savings accounts.

In summary, the laws that Congress has passed with respect to taxation of early distributions from retirement plans represent a compromise among several competing objectives, including

- encouraging employees to participate in retirement plans;
- promoting the preservation of retirement assets;
- allowing participants to have access to their retirement savings when they would otherwise face substantial economic hardship; and
- assuring that the tax preferences granted to retirement savings plans are not used for purposes other than to fund workers' financial security during retirement.

CONVERTING RETIREMENT SAVINGS INTO INCOME

A retiree who is deciding how to convert retirement savings into income will have to take into account many risks. Increases in average life expectancy mean that many retirees will have to ensure that their savings will last through a retirement that could span 30 or 40 years. Volatility in equity markets, the effects of inflation on purchasing power, and the possibility of substantial expenses for medical treatment and long-term care will further complicate this decision. Many retirees may find it more challenging to manage their financial assets in retirement than it was during their working years.[58]

There are a number of ways to convert retirement savings into income. One option is to purchase an annuity. A life annuity—also called an immediate annuity—is an insurance contract that provides regular income payments for life in return for an initial lump-sum premium. Life annuities can help protect retirees against some of the financial risks of retirement, especially longevity risk and investment risk. A life annuity pays income to the purchaser for as long as he or she lives, and in the case of a joint-and survivor annuity, for as long as the surviving spouse lives. Some annuities offer limited protection against inflation through annual increases in income; however, the annual increases must be paid for by accepting a lower initial monthly annuity income. Other annuities allow the purchaser to share in investment gains from growth in equity markets as a way to offset the effects of inflation. These annuities also require the purchaser to share in the investment losses if markets fall.

Relatively few 401(k) plans provide the opportunity for retiring workers to convert all or part of their 401(k) accounts into life annuities at retirement. Only 21% of plans offered an annuity option in 2007, down from 26% in 2000.[59] One reason few plans offer annuities is that they have proven to be unpopular in plans that offer them. Fewer than 10% of participants in plans that offer an annuity choose this option.[60] At retirement, most DC plan participants either take periodic withdrawals or roll the account balance into an IRA from which they take withdrawals.

Few people purchase life annuities for a number of reasons. Social Security provides benefits in the form of an inflation-adjusted annuity, and some retirees may consider this to be sufficient protection against the risk of spending all of their retirement assets before they die. In addition, about one-third of retirees receive income from defined benefit pensions, and they therefore have less need to purchase an annuity with their retirement savings. Some potential purchasers of annuities are concerned that the fees charged by insurers are too high and that the insurance companies do a poor job of explaining the fees that they charge. Others are concerned that purchasing an annuity will reduce the financial assets that they have available to meet unexpected expenses. Finally, some older persons prefer not to purchase an annuity in the hope that they will be able to leave their assets as an inheritance for their children. For these and other reasons, the number of retirees who purchase income annuities has remained relatively low compared with the number who elect to take periodic withdrawals from their retirement accounts.

Policy Issue: The Role of Income Annuities in Retirement

Defined benefit pension plans are required by law to offer participants a joint and survivor annuity as the default form of benefit.[61] No such requirement applies to defined contribution plans. Congress could require DC plan sponsors to contract with insurance companies to offer participants the option of taking their retirement benefits in the form of an annuity, but most policy proposals have focused on making annuities a more appealing option rather than a mandatory form of benefit. For example, H.R. 2748 of the 111th Congress (Pomeroy) would amend the Internal Revenue Code to exclude from gross income up to 50% of annuity income up to an annual maximum of $5,000 for single tax filers and $10,000 for couples filing jointly.

Because most 401(k) plans do not offer an annuity option, retirees who wish to purchase annuities have to withdraw money from their accounts and buy annuities in the individual market. Individual annuities are more expensive than group annuities, and they place the responsibility for finding the best deal from a financially sound insurer on individuals who usually have had little or no experience shopping for annuities. Many consumers may not feel competent to do this on their own. They may be more comfortable taking periodic withdrawals from their accounts. Some retirees are reluctant to purchase a life annuity because canceling the annuity contract can be costly. The charge for canceling an annuity—the "surrender charge"—can account for more than 10% of the principal in the first year of the contract.[62]

Many economists have found the low demand for life annuities to be puzzling in light of the protection they provide against longevity risk. Recent research has found that the appeal of annuities to potential purchasers depends greatly on whether prospective buyers understand and appreciate the value of the income security that annuities provide. Researchers have found that when annuities are portrayed—or "framed"—as investment vehicles, the lower rates of return on life annuities (which are backed mainly by bonds) can put them at a competitive disadvantage with respect to stocks and stock mutual funds. However, when the insurance aspects of annuities are emphasized—in particular, the insurance against outliving one's assets—potential buyers have been found to be more receptive to the idea of buying a life annuity.[63]

Automatic Trial Income

As a way to familiarize people with annuities, researchers at the Retirement Security Project have suggested a strategy they call "automatic trial income." This would allow retirees to "test drive" an annuity for 24 months.[64] They suggest that if the default form of benefit from a 401(k) plan were a monthly check, even for only a 24-month period with the option to take the remainder as a lump-sum at the end of two years – it would help change the public's perception of retirement accounts by framing them as an income stream rather than as a lump sum.

Under automatic trial income, at least part of the assets in a worker's 401(k) account would be automatically paid out as income at retirement unless the individual chooses another option. Retirees would receive monthly payments from the automatic trial income plan for 24 months, at the end of which they could choose to take the remainder as a lump sum or have it converted to an annuity. To assure that only people who are near retirement have their accounts distributed as income when they leave an employer, automatic trial income could apply only to those who are 55 or older when they leave a job. To prevent small account balances from being converted to annuities, the policy could apply only to accounts above a minimum value of perhaps $50,000.

Advanced Life Deferred Annuity

Another annuity product, the Advanced Life Deferred Annuity (ALDA) is purchased at retirement but does not begin paying income until the purchaser reaches an advanced age, such as 80 or 85. If the purchaser dies before the age at which income payments are scheduled to begin, he or she forfeits the premium. On the other hand, because income payments are deferred until an advanced age, premiums would be relatively low compared to immediate income annuities. A recent analysis concluded that "this product would provide a substantial proportion of the longevity insurance provided by an immediate annuity, at a small fraction of the cost," and that "few households would suffer significant losses were it used as a 401(k) plan default."[65] Although the ALDA could provide substantial insurance against living into very old age for a comparatively low premium, "it remains to be seen whether such a product would overcome annuity aversion."[66]

One way to help participants in 401(k) plans to begin thinking of their accounts as a source of retirement income rather than as a savings account would be to report the value of the participant's accrued benefits as a stream of monthly income beginning at age 65 in addition to reporting the account balance. To make these presentations comparable across plans, it might be necessary for the federal government to set standards on the appropriate interest rates and mortality tables for plans to use in restating account balances as streams of future income.

Some financial firms are designing managed withdrawal programs as alternatives to annuities. These are typically investment accounts with periodic distributions that are designed to assure that the account balance will not be exhausted before a specified number of years have passed. Unlike annuities, however, these accounts do not provide longevity insurance. The account owner bears the risk that investment losses or living longer than he or she anticipated will result in the account being exhausted during his or her lifetime.

CONCLUSION

About half of all workers in the United States participate in employer-sponsored retirement plans, a proportion that has remained essentially unchanged since the early 1970s. Since the 1980s, the proportion of workers in defined benefit pension plans has fallen while the proportion in defined contribution plans has risen. Sponsorship of retirement plans is substantially lower among small employers than among large employers. Efforts to increase retirement plan sponsorship among small employers have had only limited success. Some policy analysts have suggested that expanding access to payroll deduction IRAs could greatly increase the number of employees at small firms who have a retirement savings account.

Even among employers who offer a retirement plan, not all workers participate. Roughly 20% to 25% of workers employed at firms that sponsor a defined contribution plan do not participate in the plan. Participation rates may rise if more firms adopt automatic enrollment, but currently, almost two-thirds of DC plans continue to require employees to elect to participate in the plan.

On average, individual workers who participate in DC plans contribute about 6% of their pay to the plan, and households with one or more participants contribute about 5% of total household earnings. One way to boost employee savings rates would be for employers to adopt automatic escalation of contributions. Employee contributions can be increased slightly each year until reaching a target contribution rate, such as 10% of pay. As with automatic enrollment, employees must be permitted to opt out of the increase or to choose another contribution rate.

In most DC plans, workers must decide not only whether to participate in the plan and how much to contribute, but also how to invest the contributions. As employers have become more aware of how daunting these choices can be for their employees, some have begun to add life-cycle funds that automatically adjust the allocation of contributions between stocks, bonds, and other investments based on the employee's expected date of retirement. The majority of plan sponsors also offer investment education for participants. Some employers arrange for financial planners or other professionals to offer investment advice to their employees.

Excessive fees can substantially reduce retirement account balances, but plan participants often are unable to discern from their account statements how much they are paying in fees and what services they are receiving in exchange for the fees charged to their accounts. Improving the disclosure of fees charged to participants in 401(k) plans could help to drive down fees because participants and plan sponsors would be better able to compare fees across plans and to evaluate the services provided relative to the fees charged for those services.

Although pre-retirement access to money held in 401(k) plans is limited by law, money sometimes "leaks" from workers' accounts before they retire. This happens when a worker withdraws funds from a 401(k) plan when changing jobs, or through a hardship distribution from the plan. Current law imposes a 10% tax penalty on most withdrawals from 401(k) plans before age 591/2. The tax penalty creates a disincentive for withdrawing money from the account before retirement and also helps assure that 401(k) accounts remain dedicated to preparing for retirement rather than functioning as tax-deferred general-purpose savings accounts.

Workers who are approaching retirement today are less likely than those who retired 20 or more years ago to have a defined benefit pension. Those who have retirement savings in a 401(k) plan or an IRA will have to decide how to convert their retirement savings into retirement income. One of the risks that they will face is the possibility that if they withdraw money too quickly, they might exhaust their savings while they still have many years to live. Income annuities insure retirees against the possibility of outliving their retirement savings, but for a variety of reasons income annuities have not yet proved to be a popular option for providing retirement income. One of the most important public policy challenges of the next several years will be to develop strategies that will help retirees manage their retirement savings wisely so that they can remain financially independent throughout retirement.

ACKNOWLEDGMENTS

Patrick Purcell was also a co-author of this report.

End Notes

[1] Not all DC plans are 401(k) plans, but 401(k) plans hold about 67% of DC plan assets. Other DC plans include 403(b) plans for non-profit employers, 457 plans for state and local governments, and miscellaneous other DC plans. Increasingly, 403(b) plans and 457 plans operate similarly to 401(k) plans. In this report the terms "401(k)" plan and "defined contribution" plan are used interchangeably unless a distinction is noted in the text.

[2] U.S. Department of Labor, Bureau of Labor Statistics, *National Compensation Survey: Employee Benefits in Private Industry in the United States, March 2007*, Summary 07-05, August 2007. The sample represented 108 million workers.

[3] On October 11, 2007, the Standard & Poor's 500 Index of common stocks reached an intra-day high of 1,576, an all-time record for the index. On March 6, 2009, the S&P 500 fell to an intra-day low of 667, a decline of 57.7% from its all-time high. Over the next three months, stock prices climbed 41%. The S&P 500 closed at a value of 943 on June 1, 2009. This was 40% lower than the index's highest level in October 2007. By July 7, the S&P 500 had fallen to 881.

[4] Board of Governors of the Federal Reserve System, *Flow of Funds Accounts of the United States: Flows and Outstandings*, Fourth Quarter 2008, March 12, 2009, p. 113.

[5] U.S. Department of Labor, Bureau of Labor Statistics, *National Compensation Survey, March 2007*, Summary 07-05, August 2007. In contrast, the BLS data indicate that 89% of workers in state and local governments were offered a retirement plan of some kind. Eighty-three percent of state and local workers were offered a DB plan, 29% were offered a DC plan, and 23% were offered both types of plan. See *National Compensation Survey: Employee Benefits in State and Local Governments in the United States, September 2007*, Summary 08-01, March 2008.

[6] The Census Bureau data are from a CRS analysis of the March 2008 Current Population Survey (CPS). The National Compensation Survey is a survey of business establishments. The CPS is a survey of households. The CPS asks households about the number of workers employed by the firm where the respondent is employed. A firm may consist of more than one establishment. Some small establishments are operating units of larger firms.

[7] Bureau of Labor Statistics, National Compensation Survey, March 2007.

[8] CRS calculations based on analysis of the Census Bureau's March 2008 Current Population Survey.

[9] Under I.R.C. §414(q), for 2009 a highly compensated employee is anyone who owned 5% or more of the firm at any time during 2008 or 2009 or anyone whose compensation in 2009

exceeds $110,000. The employer can elect to count only workers in the top 20% of employee compensation as an HCE, but must count all 5% owners.

10 A plan must satisfy one of two tests: either the proportion of non-highly compensated employees (NHCEs) covered by the plan must be at least 70% of the proportion of highly compensated employees (HCEs) covered by the plan, or the average contribution percentage for NHCEs must be at least 70% of the average contribution percentage for HCEs. Plans that have employer matching contributions are subject to the "actual contribution percentage" (ACP) test, which measures the contribution rate to HCEs' accounts relative to the contribution rate to NHCEs' accounts.

11 The maximum annual employee salary deferral into a 401(k) plan is $16,500 in 2009 (I.R.C. §402(g)). Employees aged 50 and older can contribute an additional $5,500. The total annual addition to a 401(k) plan—comprising the sum of employer and employee contributions—is limited to $49,000 in 2009 (I.R.C. §415(c)).

12 U.S. Department of Labor, Bureau of Labor Statistics, *Employee Benefits in Small Private Establishments, 1990*, Bulletin 2388, September 1991.

13 U.S. Department of Labor, Bureau of Labor Statistics, *National Compensation Survey, March 2007*, Summary 07-05, August 2007.

14 U.S. Small Business Administration, Office of Advocacy.

15 In the 111th Congress, Sen. Jeff Bingaman introduced S. 3760, the Automatic IRA Act of 2010, which would provide for Auto IRAs. Rep. Richard Neal introduced companion legislation, H.R. 6099. Further background on the Auto IRA proposal can be found in Pursuing Universal Retirement Security Through Automatic IRAs, by J. Mark Irwy and David C. John, available at http://www.brookings.edu/papers/2009/07_automatic_ira_iwry.aspx.

16 U.S. Department of Labor, Bureau of Labor Statistics, *National Compensation Survey, March 2007*, Summary 07-05, August 2007.

17 The participation rate in 401(k) plans is from the Profit Sharing/401(k) Council of America's 51st Annual Survey of Profit Sharing and 401(k) Plans. The participation rate in DC plans of all types is from the Department of Labor's National Compensation Survey.

18 This participation rate is based on a CRS analysis of the Federal Reserve Board's 2007 Survey of Consumer Finances. Similarly, a CRS analysis of the Census Bureau's Survey of Income and Program Participation (SIPP) showed that only 30% of workers under age 35 participated in a defined contribution plan in 2006.

19 The take-up rate is calculated as the percentage of workers who participated divided by the percentage offered a plan. For workers under age 35, the take-up rate in 2007 was .318/.456 = .697.

20 All figures cited in this paragraph are from the Federal Reserve Board's 2007 Survey of Consumer Finances.

21 A notable exception to this rule is the Roth 401(k). In a Roth 401(k), the employee's salary deferrals into the plan are made with after-tax income. In retirement, the part of the withdrawals attributable to the employee's contributions and investment earnings on those contributions is tax free.

22 For more information, see CRS Report RS21795, *The Retirement Savings Tax Credit: A Fact Sheet*, by John J. Topoleski.

23 Some tax credits—such as the earned income tax credit (EITC) for low-income families—are refundable.

24 Consider, for example, a young married couple with one child, for whom the husband is the sole breadwinner. In 2007, 25% of all workers aged 18 to 34 who worked year-round, full-time had earnings of $21,000 or less. Taking into account the standard deduction in effect

for 2007 ($10,700) and three personal exemptions ($3,400 X 3 = $10,200), a couple with gross income of $21,000 would have had taxable income of $100. The child tax credit of $1,000 would reduce their tax liability to zero. For this couple, the saver's credit would have no value because it is not refundable.

[25] See, for example, CRS Report RL33116, *Retirement Plan Participation and Contributions: Trends from 1998 to 2006*, by Patrick Purcell, and CRS Report RL30922, *Retirement Savings and Household Wealth in 2007*, by Patrick Purcell.

[26] Employers often suspend the match during difficult times. According to the Pension Rights Center, between June 2008 and June 2009, nearly 300 medium and large employers had announced plans to suspend, reduce, or delay their 401(k) matching contributions.[26] See http://www.pensionrights.org/pubs/facts/401(k)-match.html#.

[27] The limit in 2009 is $16,500 (I.R.C. §415(c)).

[28] With respect to after-tax income, even non-participants in plans that do not offer a matching contribution are reducing their total income by not contributing. Nevertheless, because contributions to a 401(k) plan reduce a worker's take-home pay, some workers are willing to give up higher future retirement income for higher current income.

[29] For more information, see CRS Report RL33845, *Retirement Savings: How Much Will Workers Have When They Retire?*, by Patrick Purcell and Debra B. Whitman.

[30] This takes into account contributions by both the household head and his or her spouse. Among household heads who contributed, the median monthly contribution was $280, or $3,360 on an annual basis. This was just 22% of the maximum permissible employee salary deferral under I.R.C. §402(g) in 2007, which was $15,000.

[31] In Table 3, households are grouped by income quartile. Income includes earnings and unearned income, such as interest, dividends, rent, and transfer payments. Contributions are reported as a percentage of total household earnings.

[32] Section 902 of P.L. 109-280exempts plans with a qualified automatic contribution arrangement from the nondiscrimination tests.

[33] U.S. Department of Labor, Bureau of Labor Statistics, National Compensation Survey.

[34] ERISA §404(c). Employer stock cannot be one of the three core investment choices.

[35] Profit Sharing/401(k) Council of America, 51st Annual Survey.

[36] Profit Sharing/401(k) Council of America, 51st Annual Survey.

[37] Profit Sharing/401(k) Council of America, 44th Annual Survey and 51st Annual Survey.

[38] Section 406(a)(1)(C) of ERISA prohibits a fiduciary from engaging in a transaction when he knows or should know that such transaction constitutes a direct or indirect furnishing of goods, services, or facilities between the plan and a party in interest. Section 601 of the PPA amended §408(b) of ERISA to add an exception to the transactions prohibited by ERISA for an "eligible investment advice arrangement." For more information, see CRS Report RS22514, *Investment Advice and the Pension Protection Act of 2006*, by Jon O. Shimabukuro.

[39] 29 U.S.C. § 1108(g)(3)(B)(i)-(v).

[40] *Federal Register*, Vol. 74, No. 223, November 20, 2009, p. 60156.

[41] Under the PPA, a target date fund is a "Qualified Default Investment Alternative" (QDIA).

[42] See http://aging.senate.gov/record.cfm?id=308665.

[43] *Investment News*, "Labor Department, SEC to probe target date funds," April 3, 2009.

[44] Defined Contribution/401(k) Fee Study, Deloitte Consulting LLP, Spring 2009. The report is available on the ICI website at http://www.idc.org/pdf/rpt_09_dc_401k_fee_study.pdf.

[45] See CRS Report RL34678, *Fee Disclosure in Defined Contribution Retirement Plans: Background and Legislation*, by John J. Topoleski.

[46] The examples are based on an account with an initial balance of $20,000 growing at an average annual rate of 7.0%.

[47] Even if fees charged to a DB plan are paid for from plan assets, this increases the sponsor's funding obligation.

[48] *Federal Register*, Vol. 75, No. 135, July 16, 2010, p. 41599-41638.

[49] 26 U.S.C. §401(k)(2)(B)(i)(IV). All distributions are taxable, except any portion that is attributable to after-tax contributions. I.R.C. §72(t) lists limited cases in which distributions made before age 591/2 are not subject to the 10% additional tax on early distributions.

[50] 26 C.F.R. §1.401(k)-1(d). Regular matching contributions and discretionary profit-sharing contributions may also be distributed on account of hardship if the plan so provides. See 26 C.F.R. §1.401(k)-1(d)(3)(ii).

[51] The exceptions to the 10% additional tax are listed at 26 USC, §72(t).

[52] Loans are not permitted from IRAs, but money in an IRA can, in effect, be "borrowed" for 60 days because the law states that any distribution from an IRA that is not deposited in the same or another IRA within 60 days is a taxable distribution. (26 U.S.C. § 408(d)).

[53] More information is available in CRS Report RL30496, *Pension Issues: Lump-Sum Distributions and Retirement Income Security*, by Patrick Purcell, *Pension Issues: Lump-Sum Distributions and Retirement Income Security*, by Patrick Purcell.

[54] If the individual chooses this option, federal law requires 20% of the account balance to be withheld and forwarded to the IRS toward any income tax and tax penalties owed.

[55] Under IRC §72(t), the 10% penalty is waived if the distribution is made in a series of "substantially equal periodic payments" based on the recipient's life expectancy or if the recipient has retired from the plan sponsor at age 55 or older. Other exceptions to the 10% additional tax apply under special circumstances. See CRS Report R40192, *Early Withdrawals and Required Minimum Distributions in Retirement Accounts: Issues for Congress*, by John J. Topoleski.

[56] If the distribution is not rolled over within 60 days, the 20% withheld is applied to the taxes owed on the distribution. If the distribution is rolled over within 60 days, the 20% withheld is credited toward the income tax that the individual owes for the year. If the participant has received the distribution in cash, then to roll over the full amount of the distribution, the recipient must have access to other funds that are at least equal to 20% withheld by the employer.

[57] Distributions of $5,000 or more require the participant's written consent. The $5,000 limit was established by the Taxpayer Relief Act of 1997 (P.L. 105-34). The amount had been set at $3,500 by Retirement Equity Act of 1984. It was originally established at $1,750 by ERISA in 1974.

[58] For more information, see CRS Report R40008, *Converting Retirement Savings into Income: Annuities and Periodic Withdrawals*, by Janemarie Mulvey and Patrick Purcell.

[59] Profit Sharing/401(k) Council of America, 51st Annual Survey.

[60] Hewitt Associates, survey of 401(k) plans, various years.

[61] ERISA § 205; 29 USC § 1055.

[62] Typically, surrender charges drop by about one percentage point per year, eventually allowing penalty-free withdrawals from the annuity.

[63] See "Why Don't People Insure Late Life Consumption? A Framing Explanation of the Under-Annuitization Puzzle," by J. R. Brown, J. R. Kling, S. Mullainathan, and M. V. Wrobel, TIAA-CREF Institute, April 2008.

[64] See *Increasing Annuitization in 401(k) Plans with Automatic Trial Income* by William Gale, J. Mark Iwry, David C. John, and Lina Walker at

http://www.retirementsecurityproject.org/pubs/File/RSP_TrialIncomev4(2).pdf.

[65] Guan Gong and Anthony Webb, *Evaluating the Advanced Life Deferred Annuity*, Boston College Center for Retirement Research, Working Paper no. 2007-15, September 2007.

[66] Ibid.

In: Managed 401(k) Accounts
Editor: Harold Parker
ISBN: 978-1-63463-592-9

Chapter 3

FEE DISCLOSURE IN DEFINED CONTRIBUTION RETIREMENT PLANS*

John J. Topoleski

SUMMARY

As households become more reliant on 401(k) plans and other defined contribution pension plans for future retirement income, policymakers have become more concerned that participants could be unaware of the fees charged in their plans. Small differences in fees charged can have large impacts on account balances upon retirement. This report provides information on the kinds of fees that are charged in 401(k) and other defined contribution plans.

* This is an edited, reformatted and augmented version of a Congressional Research Service report (RL34678) originally entitled Fee Disclosure in Defined Contribution Retirement Plans: Background and Legislation, issued January 7, 2011.

BACKGROUND ON 401(K) FEES

The Structure of 401(k) Plans and the Impact of Fees

Defined contribution (DC) plans are employer-sponsored retirement plans in which employees or employers, or both, contribute to an individual employee's account that accrues investment returns.[1] Upon retirement, employees use the accounts as a source of income. DC plans may be "qualified" if they meet certain Internal Revenue Service (IRS) guidelines with respect to pension plan contributions, benefits, and distributions. 401(k) plans are qualified plans that include a cash or deferred arrangement under which participants can choose to contribute part of their before-tax compensation to the plan rather than receive the compensation in cash.[2] The tax code allows employees to contribute a pre-tax maximum of $15,500 in 2008 to their individual 401(k) accounts. Although there are other kinds of DC account plans in addition to 401(k) plans (such as 457 plans for employees of state or local governments and 403(b) plans for educational institutions and other tax-exempt organizations), these plans operate similarly to 401(k) plans, and the term 401(k) plan often refers to these other plans as well.[3] Unless specifically stated, the term 401(k) plan in this report also refers to these other plans.

The percentage of employees covered by DC plans has been increasing in recent years. According to the National Compensation Survey from the Bureau of Labor Statistics, 36% of all workers participated in a DC plan in 1999. This percentage increased to 43% by 2006. DC plans will continue to play an important role in Americans' retirement security.

Some have raised concerns about the fees that participants in 401(k) plans are charged. Small differences in fees can yield large differences in account balances at retirement, especially in the case of yearly or recurring fees.[4] For example, *Table 1* shows the effect that a 0.5%, a 1.0%, and a 1.5% annual fee would have on an initial $20,000 account balance that earns 7% yearly. After 20 years, the account would have about $77,000 if no fee is charged, whereas the account would have about $70,000 if a 0.5% fee is charged. The account would have a balance of about $58,000 if a 1.5% fee is charged (17% less than the account that charged a 0.5% fee). If a 1.5% annual fee is charged, over the course of 30 years an account holder would pay more than $52,000 in fees. The complexity of 401(k) plan arrangements may provide opportunities for fees to be higher than they otherwise might be, particularly if plan sponsors and participants are not fully informed of the fees they pay. Policies that increase the transparency of fee arrangements may result in participants paying lower fees.

Table 1. Effect of Annual Fees on a $20,000 Balance (Assuming 7.0% Annual Real Rate of Return) (amount in $)

		Annual Fee		
Account Balance	None	0.5%	1.0%	1.5%
After 20 years After 30 years	77,394 152,245	70,473 132,287	64,143 114,870	58,355 99,679

Source: CRS calculations.

Note: The average annual real rate of return on the Standard & Poor's 500 Stock Market Index from 1926 to 2007 was 6.99%.

Under the Employee Retirement Income Security Act (ERISA; P.L. 93-406), plan sponsors have a fiduciary responsibility to plan participants; that is, they must carry out their responsibilities prudently and solely in the interest of the plan's participants.[5] Among other duties, fiduciaries have a responsibility in ERISA to defray reasonable expenses of administering the plan, but there are limited fee disclosure requirements to plan participants.[6]

Structure of 401(k) Plans

Figure 1 details the structure of a typical 401(k) plan, although particular plans may have slightly different structures. Fee arrangements affect three groups in 401(k) plans: (1) plan participants, (2) plan sponsors and plan administrators, and (3) service providers. The plan participants are the employees of the company who have individual accounts to which the employees, the employer, or both contribute. As the plan sponsor, the employer arranges for one or more service providers to provide various services for the plan. Prior to choosing a service provider, plan sponsors might ask several providers for details on the products they offer and the fees they charge. Service providers provide a number of services for plan sponsors and participants including the day-to-day plan business such as recording transactions, arranging for loans, cashing out retirees' accounts, and arranging for investment options. Most service providers offer several mutual funds to the retirement plan and may offer other investment options as well, including insurance company offerings such as variable annuities and bank or trust company pooled investment trusts.

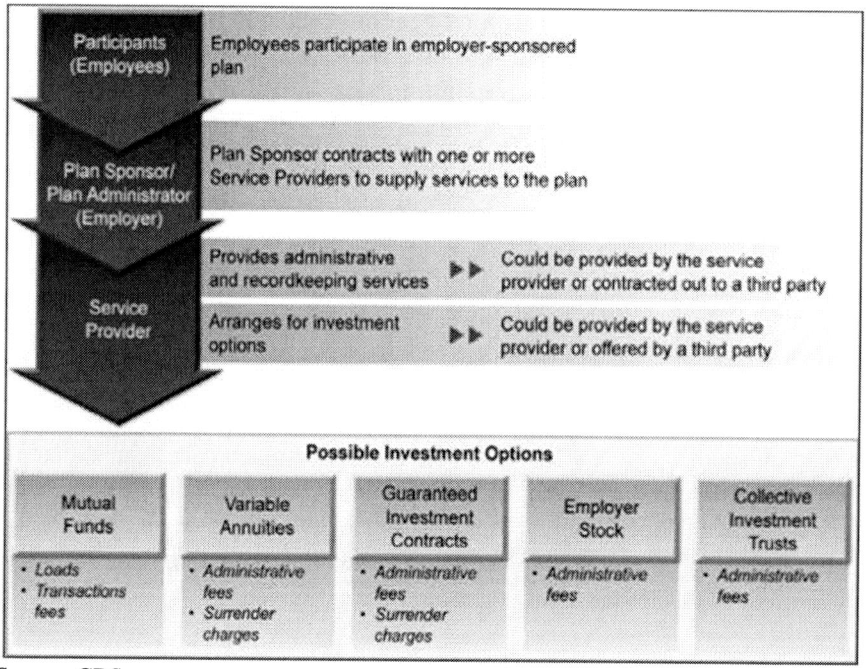

Source: CRS.

Figure 1. Structure of a Typical Defined Contribution Plan.

Employers could purchase these services separately from individual service providers or employers could purchase two or more services from a single service provider in a *bundled* arrangement. In a bundled arrangement, a service provider offers several services or investment alternatives to the plan for a single fee. The service provider may contract out the provision of these services to one or more third parties. Current law does not require the services in bundled arrangements to be priced separately. The Department of Labor (DOL) has issued regulations to require service providers to identify all parties who receive payments of more than $5,000 from the plan.[7]

The terms *plan sponsor* and *plan administrator* are often used interchangeably, although they need not be the same entity. A plan sponsor is an employer that establishes a retirement plan. The plan administrator is responsible for the day to day running of the plan. The plan administrator may be the employer, a committee of employees, a company executive, or someone hired for that purpose. The plan administrator is defined in 26 U.S.C. § 414(g) as the person specifically so designated by the terms of the plan or the employer in the absence of such a designation. To avoid confusion, this report's use of the term *plan sponsor* includes *plan administrator*.

In most DC plans, participants have control over some or all of the assets in their individual accounts, although this control is limited to the investment options made available by the service providers. Less common are plans in which the participants have no control over the assets.

Current proposals in Congress would require plan sponsors of all DC plans to receive fee disclosures from service providers, but only participants in plans in which the participants exercise control over the assets would receive fee disclosures from plan sponsors. *Table 2* indicates that 401(k) plans where the employee has control over all or a portion of the assets in the plan accounted for 88.8% of all DC plans in 2005.

Table 2. Number of Defined Contribution Plans and Participants, by Size of Plan and Extent of Participant Direction of Investments, 2006

		All Plans	*Plans With 2 - 99 Participants*	*Plans with 100 or More Participants*
	Number of Plans	451,993	389,793	62,200
All Plans	Number of Participants (in thousands)	58,352	7,955	50,397
	Number of Plans	383,442	325,980	57,462
Participant Directs All Investments	Number of Participants (in thousands)	46,674	6,999	39,675
	Number of Plans	19,672	17,114	2,558
Participant Directs Portion of Assets	Number of Participants (in thousands)	8,693	325	8,368
	Number of Plans	48,882	46,700	2,182
Participant Does Not Direct Any Investments	Number of Participants (in thousands)	2,984	631	2,353

Source: U.S. Department of Labor, Table D-6 of Private Pension Plan Bulletin, Abstract of 2006 Form 5500 Annual Reports.

Notes: Table does not include plans that did not report the number of participants. Employers may have multiple plans. Employees may be in multiple plans and are counted in each plan in which they participate. The small discrepancies in the totals for each column are found in the original source.

One of the proposals in Congress (S. 401) would provide assistance to small employers (employers with less than 100 employees) by providing educational and compliance materials to small employers and by providing assistance with finding and understanding affordable investment options. *Table 2* indicates that 13.9% of plan participants are in plans in which there are fewer than 100 participants.

Types of 401(k) Fees

The Employee Benefits Security Administration (EBSA) is an agency within DOL. It is charged with protecting the integrity of employee benefits, including retirement plans. An EBSA publication, *A Look At 401(k) Plan Fees*, describes three types of fees: plan administration fees, investment-related fees, and individual service fees.[8] According to EBSA, investment-related fees are the largest component of 401(k) plan fees.

Plan Administration Fees

These are fees for the day-to-day operations of plans such as record keeping, accounting, legal, and trustee services. Additional services might also be provided, such as access to customer service representatives, educational seminars, or daily valuation. The amount charged for administrative fees can vary depending on the quantity and quality of the services offered. For example, service providers that offer website access with extensive online services might charge higher fees than service providers that provide only basic website services. Administrative fees may be charged either as a flat fee per participant or as a percentage of plan assets.

Investment Fees

Investment fees cover the costs of transactions within investment options, such as the trades a particular mutual fund makes. Some investment fees include the following.

- *Sales Charges:* These are also known as loads. A front-end load is charged upon investing in some mutual funds. Front-end loads reduce the amount of the initial investment. Back-end loads (also called deferred sales charges or redemption fees) are charged upon selling mutual funds.

- *Marketing and Distribution Fees:* These are called "Rule 12b-1" fees after the 1980 Securities and Exchange Commission's (SEC) rule that allowed mutual funds to charge for marketing and distribution of mutual fund shares.[9] Rule 12b-1 fees are annual fees that may be charged by mutual funds from fund assets to pay for promotional costs and commissions to brokers and other salespeople. A point of contention is that service providers may receive 12b-1 fees for including particular mutual funds as investment options for participants in the plans they administer. Although the SEC does not limit the amount of 12b-1 fees, under the Financial Industry Regulatory Authority (FINRA) rules, 12b-1 fees that are used to pay marketing and distribution expenses (as opposed to shareholder service expenses) cannot exceed 0.75% of a fund's average net assets per year.
- *Soft Dollar Fees:* These payments are for brokerage firm services (such as research) other than commissions for trade execution.
- *Surrender and Transfer Charges:* These are fees that insurance companies may charge when employers withdraw from variable annuities before the contract expires.
- *Wrap Fee:* Wrap fees are "all-in-one" fees that combine asset management, financial planning, and brokerage services together for one fee.

Individual Service Fees

Individuals are charged fees that are associated with using optional features in a 401(k) plan, such as loan origination fees and fees for hardship withdrawals.

Documents Required by Current Law

Three documents required by current law contain information about potential fees: Summary Plan Descriptions (SPDs), Summary Annual Reports, and Account statements.

Summary Plan Descriptions

SPDs describe how plans operate.[10] Plan sponsors are required to automatically provide copies of these documents to plan participants upon enrollment and upon written request of plan participants. Among other items, SPDs contain information about eligibility and vesting requirements, plan benefits, and the source of contributions. SPDs are required to disclose a summary of provisions that may result in a fee charged to a participant, the payment of which is a condition to the receipt of benefits under the plan. An EBSA Field Assistance Bulletin notes that charges for hardship withdrawals, if a plan allows hardship withdrawals, might be an example of such a charge.[11]

Plans must also make a Summary of Material Modifications available within seven months of the end of the plan year in which significant changes to the plan were made.

Annual Report Form 5500

The Form 5500 was jointly developed by DOL, the IRS, and the Pension Benefit Guaranty Corporation (PBGC) and is required to be submitted annually by ERISA-covered plans. This annual report contains various schedules with information on the financial condition, investments, and operations of the plans. On November 16, 2007, EBSA issued regulations to revise the Form 5500. Among other requirements, the regulations require administrators and sponsors of plans with more than 100 participants to disclose the identity of service providers who receive direct or indirect compensation of $5,000 or greater in connection with services rendered to the plan.[12] The types of compensation include 12b-1 fees, brokerage commissions, and soft dollars. A plan's annual report may be available from the employer upon request and is available from DOL in the EBSA Public Disclosure Facility.

Benefit Statements

Section 508 of the Pension Protection Act of 2006 (P.L. 109-280) requires plan sponsors to provide participants in DC plans with quarterly benefit statements if the investments are participant-directed and annual statements if the investments are not participant-directed. The quarterly benefit statement must include the value of each investment in the individual's account, an explanation of any limitations or restrictions on any right of the participant or beneficiary under the plan to direct an investment, and an explanation of the importance of a well-balanced and diversified investment portfolio for long-term retirement security. On July 23, 2008, DOL issued proposed regulations that would require plan fiduciaries to disclose to participants, on a quarterly basis, the actual dollar amount charged to the participant's account during the preceding quarter for individual services (such as fees for processing plan loans).[13]

FEE DISCLOSURE LEGISLATION

Four bills introduced in the 111th Congress address the expenses and fees charged in 401(k) and other DC plans. H.R. 2779, H.R. 2989, H.R. 4146, and S. 401 would have required service providers to disclose to plan sponsors the services to be provided to the plan and the expected fees and expenses. The disclosures would have had to be made prior to entering into a contract for services to a plan and upon any material changes to the contract for services. The bills would also have required plan sponsors to disclose to a participant the expected fees and expenses associated with the plan and the plan's investment options. This disclosure would have had to be made prior to any initial contribution by a participant. Plan sponsors would also have had to provide, on a regular basis, each participant with details of the fees and expenses the participant incurred over a specified period.

The following paragraphs summarize the bills. Following the summaries, the report describes the bills' details in the following categories: (1) disclosures from service providers to plan sponsors, (2) disclosures from plan sponsors to plan participants, (3) a minimum investment option, (4) assistance to small employers, (5) enforcement and review, and (6) imposition of taxes.

Bill Summaries H.R. 2989 and S. 401

Representative George Miller introduced H.R. 2989, the 401(k) Fair Disclosure and Pension Security Act of 2009, on April 21, 2009.[14] H.R. 2989 would have (1) required greater disclosure of fees paid in 401(k) plans, (2) provided for independent investment advice for participants in DC plans, and (3) provided temporary funding relief to defined benefit plans. This bill was reported out of the House Education and Labor Committee on June 24, 2009, by a vote of 29 - 17. Senator Tom Harkin introduced S. 401, the Defined Contribution Fee Disclosure Act of 2009, on February 9, 2009. In many respects, S. 401 and the fee disclosure provisions of H.R. 2989 are similar.[15]

The provisions in H.R. 2989 that would have required greater disclosure of 401(k) fees and S. 401 would have amended ERISA and would have required.

End Notes

[1] A defined contribution plan is defined in 26 U.S.C. § 414(i) as "a plan which provides for an individual account for each participant and for benefits based solely on the amount contributed to the participant's account, and any income, expenses, gains and losses, and any forfeitures of accounts of other participants which may be allocated to such participant's account."

[2] The names for the various types of defined contribution retirement plans are often the section of the Internal Revenue Code that authorizes these plans (e.g., 26 U.S.C. 401(k) or 26 U.S.C. 457(b)).

[3] See 26 U.S.C. § 402(g)(1).

[4] For a detailed analysis of the effects that fees have on account balances, see CRS Report RL34213, Retirement Savings Accounts: Fees, Expenses, and Account Balances, by Patrick Purcell.

[5] For more information, see CRS Report RL34443, Summary of the Employee Retirement Income Security Act (ERISA), by Patrick Purcell and Jennifer Staman.

[6] See 29 U.S.C. § 1104(a)(1)(A)(ii).

[7] See Department of Labor, "Annual Reporting and Disclosure," 72 Federal Register 221, November 16, 2007, pp. 64710-64730.

[8] Available at http://www.dol.gov/ebsa/pdf/401kFeesEmployee.pdf.

[9] Prior to the adoption of Rule 12b-1, the SEC generally took the view that section 12b-1 of the Investment Companies Act of 1940 (15 U.S.C. § § 80a-1 - 80a-64) prohibited mutual funds from using fund assets to pay for the sale of their shares.

[10] See 29 CFR § 2520.103-2 and 29 CFR § 2520.103-3 for regulations concerning the style and contents of SPDs.

[11] See Field Assistance Bulletin 2003-3 issued by EBSA on May 19, 2003.

[12] See Department of Labor, "Annual Reporting and Disclosure," 72 Federal Register 221, November 16, 2007, pp. 64710-64857.

[13] See Department of Labor, "Fiduciary Requirements for Disclosure in Participant-Directed Individual Account Plans," 73 Federal Register 142, July 23, 2008, pp. 43013-43044.

[14] Representative Miller introduced H.R. 1984, the 401(k) Fair Disclosure for Retirement Security Act of 2009, on April 21, 2009. H.R. 1984 was passed by the subcommittee on Health, Employment, Labor and Pensions of the House Education and Labor Committee on June 17, 2009, by a vote of 13 – 8. The provisions of this bill were included in H.R. 2989.

[15] In the 110th Congress Representative Miller introduced H.R. 3185, the 401(k) Fair Disclosure for Retirement Security Act of 2007, on July 26, 2007. H.R. 3185 was approved by the House Education and Labor Committee on April 16, 2007, and was similar to H.R. 1984. Senator Harkin introduced S. 2473, the Defined Contribution Fee Disclosure Act of 2007, on December 13, 2007. S. 2473 was nearly identical to S. 401. Representative Neal introduced H.R. 3765, the Defined Contribution Plan Fee Transparency Act of 2007, on October 4, 2007.

INDEX

D

E

F

G

H

I

L

M

N

O

P

Q

R

S

T

U

V

W

Y